Spotlight

Spotlight on Life

Brig Pabitra Chakravarti (Retd.)

ZORBA BOOKS

ZORBA BOOKS
Published by Zorba Books, June 2022

Website: www.zorbabooks.com
Email: info@zorbabooks.com
Author Name & Copyright © Brig Pabitra Chakravarti
Title:- Spotlight on Life

Printbook ISBN :- 978-93-93029-66-9
Ebook ISBN :- 978-93-93029-74-4

Zorba Books Pvt. Ltd. (opc)
Sushant Arcade,
Next to Courtyard Marriot,
Sushant Lok 1, Gurgaon – 122009, India

To my wife Narayani, daughter Bashuli, grandson Parth and son in law Pushkar.

Contents

Acknowledgements

The idea of this book was conceived while sipping a cup of hot Nilgiri tea sitting in Wellington Gymkhana Club over looking the blue mountains. My wife Narayani suggested that all my articles written and published in newspapers, magazines, social media and journals be compiled and published as a book. It was a daunting task as I took to writing on retirement twenty two years ago and the articles were scattered in different places. Compiling the articles into a book was tedious, laborious and tiring. The process brought on many highs and lows and if it had not been for Narayani who bravely suffered these moods of mine and continuously encouraged, motivated and gave valuable advice this book would not have been here today.

Dr Gaurangi Maitra my sister in law with the Tezpur University and a professional editor who has wide reading experience was able to do all the editorial work and give me valuable advice in formulating the contents and doing much of the technical work. My deep gratitude and thanks to her.

Introduction

The changing pattern of human behavior and attitude has always interested me. Over the years this interest grew given the scope of serving in the Indian Army, in India and abroad in war and in peace. It gave me the opportunity to meet people from all walks of life and observe their reaction to different situations. Thus the idea of this book was born.

On retirement twenty two years ago I began speaking on life and attitude in corporates, army institutions, educational institutions, seminars and forums. My articles have been published in newspapers, magazines and journals. This book " Spotlight on life '' incorporates my insight on human behavior, character building, valour and more importantly attitude towards life. This collection of articles is based on my real life experiences spanning six decades and my insight into different age groups, the generation gap, retired people and their ability to adapt to the journey called life.

Brig Pabitra Chakravarti

Race

The realization dawned that my whole life had been spent in a rat race.

As a young boy I am sitting with my parents in Turf Club Pune in the stands overlooking the race track. Today is the Southern Command trophy, a prestigious, high prize money race. The elite and rich come to put their money on the race. I am with my parents on invitation and the stalls were packed to capacity. The excitement grew as the horses came out and are guided to their respective stalls. All of them are thoroughbreds, owned by the rich, bold, and famous; each one ridden by an experienced high-profile jockey. The horses are impatient for the barriers to be lifted and for the race to begin. The flag came down, the horses surged forward, and the commentary started. It is a mile long race and the horses have entered the last lap. The crowd stands up, a few on benches, some looking through binoculars, the commentary rises to a crescendo, the cheering is deafening! The race is over, and some people are hugging each other with joy! Some are slumped down on their seats, tears in their eyes, dejection and frustration written all over their faces. As a young boy, I am seeing raw emotions for the first time, at close quarters. I had just seen my first *race*! We went home with much jubilation. My father who never played the races had bet a very small amount, and won ₹25,000! On the way home, our first stop

1

was the mandir (temple), and then our favorite mithai (sweet) shop to buy 'rasogollas' and 'sandesh'.

Years went by, and I became a teenager. It was the inter school sports day and I was running the last lap of the 1500 meters race. My head screamed faster, faster, faster, sweat rolled down my face, every sinew in my body strained, my lungs were crying for air, and emotions were running high, *I had to win!* As a small boy I had seen my first race and now, I had run my own *first race*!

As time went on, my life became a series of races. Races at the workplace, outrun the next man, garner promotions, and amass more money. More clients, more international travel, day calls, night calls, balancing time spent at work, and with family. Perpetually racing, racing against time. Races on the social front; must get the latest iPhone, MacBook Air laptop, home theatre for movies, and the Bose music system. Social gatherings, parties to be attended and returned, only single malt whisky, and that too, only the best to be served. Branded clothes and watches were just the tip of the iceberg, in an incessant meltdown against the latest brands. No time for leisurely weekends, and of course medical checkups could always be postponed, a sheer paucity of time! While still in your forties, high blood pressure, high levels of cholesterol and diabetes crept in. The waist line increased in tandem with the number of races.

Not just my own races, but races for my child had to be run. The child must come first in class; must keep up with the Jones, whose child goes to four coaching classes. Therefore, my child cannot join less than the four mandatory coaching classes in academics, sports, art, and music. In today's world to succeed, one has to be an all-rounder. During the school summer vacation, one must go on an international vacation. After all, the Jones go without fail; and not to Thailand or Singapore, that, is far too common and mundane. But to some exotic destination, which is aspirational, grabs the attention, and captivates our friends while dinning out!

Finally, the day came when I felt that all my responsibilities had been met. Child educated, married and settled, enough kept aside for a rainy day for my wife. Maybe, it was time to retire. I looked back on my life, and was aghast to see that my life has been full of only races! All that I can tell Saint Peter is that I ran *races;* nothing, just nothing, on the sands of time! I settled down in a sedate retired people's colony; but in spite of my best intentions, I still could not get away from races. My retired colleagues are forever talking how busy their children are, about their back to back meetings, their past glories and bravados. After some time, I too joined the fray. When the number of birthday greetings received became a race on my retired officers email group, it was the final straw! ***The realization dawned that my whole life had been spent in a rat race.*** God, please keep me out of *rat races* in my next life, and help me lead a meaningful life.

The Ten Meter Board Jump

It all starts with the Ten Meter Board Jump! We learn to believe in ourselves. It teaches us whatever the odds, we can do it!

The Eighth Corps Commander's meeting was held a few days ago. Meetings at different levels have been going on since June 2020. Since then, there have been multiple intrusions forcing more and more deployment of troops. A large number of Indian officers and men stand eyeball to eyeball with the PLA (Peoples Liberation Army) at the LAC (Line of actual control). Twenty of our jawans (soldiers) have lost their lives, and seventy six were wounded in the Galwan stand-off with China. There is no indication of a solution. Winter is setting in and presents a daunting challenge with freezing, bone numbing temperatures going down to minus forty degrees. Families, small children left far, far, away, in these Covid-19 times, without knowing when they will meet them again. The first page of the Times of India, in bold capitals announces that one officer and three men killed in a terrorist encounter near Srinagar. Their families are left devastated. These are occurrences which the Indian Army faces daily and are in the newspapers every day. What is it that makes the officers and men overcome, fear, self-doubt; cultivate the ability to withstand treacherous terrain, and inhuman climatic conditions? How are they made into men of steel? How are qualities of courage, fortitude, patience, and sacrifice, developed?

It all starts with the Ten Meter Board Jump. The steam engine of the Military Special train trudged into Kirkee station bellowing smoke. We were all sixteen year old boys, carrying our steel trunk on our head, we got into an army truck and headed to the National Defence Academy. Here in the next three years, we would be turned from raw sixteen olds to men of steel, to face the enemy's bullets and defend our country. It was a Sunday; and we were told that on the coming Sunday we would be jumping from a height of 10 meters (thirty-five feet) in full combat dress including boots, into the water. Those of us, who could not swim, should jolly well learn to swim by then!

Can I do it? This thought constantly nagged us; what if I chicken out? Doubt is the first thing to be removed from a soldier's mind. This doubt is laced with fear and lack of self-confidence. A dangerous cocktail, and a recipe for sure failure. The fateful day comes. We reach the swimming pool at 7 AM dressed in combat dress riding our cycles. Our academy numbers are called out one by one and we take the leap; 4634, 4635 and then I hear my number 4636. I climb up the steps slowly and steadily not allowing any trace of fear to show. My father an army man had drummed it into me from childhood "jak pran, thak maan", (in Bengali it means, you can lose your life, but not your self-respect) I take the plunge, emerge from the water, swim the breadth and climb out. We return to our cabins, a notch closer to becoming soldiers of the Indian Army. We had begun attaining self-confidence, eliminating fear and doubt, and believing, "we can do it!" The Ten Meter Board Jump had inculcated in us green horns the first essence of Officer Like Qualities. Qualities without which our country cannot be defended, our men cannot be led into battle to face bullets and if required, death.

The Ten Meter Board Jump was like the first steps a baby takes when learning how to walk. Thereafter there were many, many more; crossing the barbed wired double ditch, or galloping bare back on a frisky horse through Death Lane, with multiple high jumps. To inculcate grit and determination, the 20 km night route march, through difficult terrain in restricted time was undertaken. This was the grit and determination which Maj Cardoza (later Maj Gen) was able to summon, to cut off one leg with his khukri (machete), to prevent gangrene from setting in. It allowed him to lead the men in his company when engaged in fierce combat with the enemy in 1971 war, instead of being evacuated for medical help. Subsequently young officers and men undergo the Commando course with a water jump from sixty feet, force march of 40 km, survival exercise where you live off the land by catching and eating snakes and the like. The rigorous training at the National Defence Academy is at the core of the unimaginable bravery and courage of the many heroes of the Indian Army.

Today, at this very moment, there are hundreds of young officers and men on our borders, spending Diwali without their families, on the Indo-China border and facing terrorists in Jammu &Kashmir. They are defending the honour of their country at the cost of their lives. These men who are tough as nails and have nerves of steel have been moulded by the Officers Academies and Regimental Training Centers. *It all starts with the Ten Meter Board Jump! We learn to believe in ourselves. It teaches us whatever the odds, we can do it!*

Musings of a Grandfather

My daughter now has a son and I am a grandfather, life has certainly come a full circle.

One of my dreams was to become a grandfather. I felt grandfathers are elevated to a higher status. A category where you are considered to have seen life, become wise and mature. A platform from where you could look down on others with a smile as if to say, 'well, you have a long way to go!' Grandparents are a special breed. They talk endlessly about their grandchildren with an all-knowing look in their eyes. Many a time in the company of my colleagues I would feel conscious that I didn't quite belong, just because I was not a grandfather.

I had done my bit. I was father of a lovely, caring, suitably married daughter. Now all I could do was to wait and yearn for the day when I would be granted the much cherished title of a grandfather. After a long patient wait of many years, when I had reconciled and accepted my fate of being just a father, a lesser mortal; came the breaking news. I was to become a grandfather, just a few months more!

From that day my sedate, retired life took a different turn. There were constant trips from Bangalore to Hong Kong where my daughter lives. I put aside all my novels, and was submerged in literature on pregnancy, new born babies, and grand parenting. The red-letter day dawned on a bitterly cold and foggy morning at Matilda Hospital, in Hong Kong. Parth my grandson had arrived and I was a grandfather! Since that day I have spent hours sitting and just gazing at my grandson as he grew from being a few days old, to weeks, months, and years. The bond and love between us only strengthened with time. He has brought me abundant joy and happiness! He is now ten and my world revolves round him. Not a day passes when my wife and I don't spend time talking about him.

As I sit in my study surrounded by photographs, my memory goes back to the years past. The joy at the arrival of our lovely daughter, and the happy years bringing her up. The exuberance of youth, the surge of energy in sporting, and the outdoor activities. Not a care in the world about health and age. My daughter now has a son and I am a grandfather, life certainly has come a full circle. As I walk around Discovery Bay, a resort in Hong Kong, where my daughter lives, my grandson holding my hand, I see the tennis and squash courts buzzing with activity. I recollect the thrilling moments I have lived on such courts. Now the spirit is willing but the flesh feels weak. It is the time of the younger generation, our children.

The past decades have brought with it a wealth of experience. The understanding that relationships, love, and sacrifice are supreme. They bring an untold font of joy and happiness. The golden years give us ample time to invest in relationships with spouse, children, grandchildren, relatives, friends, even strangers; and feel a sense of fulfilment in our lives. The choice is ours to invest or not in these years.

Bacha Saab

I should impress her by taking her for
the movie in my Centurion tank!!

I joined the Regiment in January 1966 after the 1965 war, which was still stationed across the border in a village named Gang. On reaching Jammu the Nearest Railway Station to the Regiment, I was received by 2/Lt Arvind Kumar. He informed me that the Regiment's field location was several hours away. Arvind also added that before joining the regimental routine, it was necessary that we see a cabaret in Jammu that evening. It was indeed a colorful beginning to a happy innings in the 16 Light Cavalry! In April 1966 (if my memory serves me right), we moved back to the Indian side, and camped in a village named Jhanglot, before loading our tanks onto the rolling stock, and moving to Sangrur in Punjab.

By this time the lady wives had joined us, and having joined recently, I had not met any of them. One Sunday morning while at the Officers' Mess, I was informed by Gopi the mess waiter, that the ladies desired to meet the 'bacha saab' in the ladies room, where they had assembled for the regular Sunday dosa lunch. Having been through the National Defence Academy, I knew that I was in for a bit of good humored teasing. On entering the ladies room, I was greeted by a well planned chorus of "Oh how cute!"

My spontaneous response of "Maam, can I then sit on your lap?" was received in the true 16 Cavalry ladies spirit, and I knew I had passed their test! I was just twenty years old, and then onwards, treated by the ladies as the Regimental baby; and became a regular invitee for dinners, in the married officer's homes. We had a wonderful fun loving lot of ladies, Mrs Salochana Krishnamurthy, Meena Puri, Shoroni Choudhury, Indu Dandekar, Sakuntala Issar, Kamy Nath and Neelam Dewan. Kind and generous to a fault, they were all women of accomplishment and substance. Mrs Salochana Krishnamurthy is settled in Bangalore *and for her I still remain the 'bacha saab', even post retirement.*

A few weeks later I was sitting glum and dejected in the mess bar all alone. In walked my squadron 2IC Capt Surendra Nath, who had earlier been my Div officer in the National Defence Academy. Seeing me look dejected, he coaxed me to tell him what ailed me. I said I want to take my girlfriend for a movie, but my scooter has broken down! In the typical Capt Surendra Nath and cavalry style he said, that the Moti cinema being next door, *I should impress her by taking her for the movie in my Centurion tank!! That was the cavalry of 55 years ago!*

Going for dinner to Capt Wendy Dewan, our Adjutant; meant sitting through hours of listening to in graphic detail, how he had scored the winning goal, in football finals against the Hodson Horse Regiment. I still don't know whether it was to impress me or his newly married wife. Last year during his visit to Bangalore we met for dinner. Neelam and I pounced on him the moment we realized Wendy had started on the goal scoring story again. Poor

Wendy had forgotten that Neelam was no longer his newly wed wife or I, the twenty year old subaltern!

I was lucky to be taught, pampered and looked after during my earlier years in the regiment by officers, ladies and most of all the men. Thank you, 16 Light Cavalry!

Is Virtual Replacing Real?

Are we harming our children by over exposing them to technology during their most impressionable years?

I live in an Army Welfare Housing Organisation colony. These colonies were made for Army personnel to settle in after retirement. Naturally all my friends are retired, and grandparents. Conversations centre mainly about our children and grandchildren. When I go to my daughter, son in law and grandson in Hong Kong I get the opportunity to meet the present generation. Many of the evenings are spent out at restaurants accompanied by the young children. After being comfortably seated, the mothers will dive into their handbags and emerge with iPads, screening serials of Kunfu Panda, Simba the Lion King, Angry Birds, or any other, to cater to demands of their children. Next in line to be retrieved and placed on the table are smart phones, like miniature oxygen tanks carried everywhere by emphysema patients. Every minute, the arrival of new messages must be unfailingly and discreetly checked on these phones.

I see kids as young as 2 years plus, spend excessive time with screens and devices, watching cartoons or playing games. A boy of ten told me he plays golf at a handicap of six; I was very impressed till I realised later he was referring to golf on his gaming device. The young lad would be in for a surprise on stepping onto a real golf course. Parents feel their children are becoming smarter by learning how to count, sing, dance, study on devices. Yet, they are unable to do the simple additions, subtractions, multiplications, divisions, leave alone simple square roots without opening the calculator on the mobile. Grandparents proudly and loudly tell me that the grandchildren today are far smarter than our children or us. They can play around with devices and write projects using Google.

While browsing through old magazines at the Rajendra Singhji Army Officers Institute RSI in Bangalore, I saw on the 16th November, 2016 issue of the "TIME" a picture of a teenage girl. She has shoulder length dark hair, is wearing jeans and a pink lace shirt. She looks like all the life has been drained out of her, and she has no hope left in the world. Next to the teenage girl is the headline "Anxiety, Depression and the present Youth." Why is this happening to our children across the world? Why is drug abuse so rampant on school and college campuses? Why are dropouts on the increase? Why were so many young lives lost to the Blue Whale wave? Are the bears, lions, and zebras which we as children saw in zoos, being replaced by Kunfu Panda, Simba the Lion King, and Angry Bird on screens? Is this at the cost of young parents getting more "Me Time" for themselves? Is the real world being replaced by the virtual, and becoming increasingly more dangerous by believing that virtual experiences equal real experiences?

Our parents showed us the way to play with our friends under the blue sky of God's beautiful world. We played outdoor games and not games on devices. We went to the zoo and on picnics with our grandparents by the riverside. We had the thrill of writing projects after experimenting, and experiencing; not just an unthinking download from Google. We did not know fast food, and never thought about hypertension or diabetes till we crossed sixty. Children wearing spectacles were a rarity. We had values of integrity, honesty, loyalty instilled in us. There was no net to sneak into to see porn. We have raised a family and lived happily.

Yet, I am a great admirer of technology that has brought with it tremendous benefits. I personally make an all out effort to learn and use technology to my advantage. Even today, at the age of seventy five, I spend one hour every evening from 6 to 7 PM with a tutor, improving my knowledge and skill set of the computer and devices. At the same time, we must take all precautions to guard against the evils that technology brings with it. We should be able analyse with an open mind the misuse of screens and devices.

I feel that young parents and we grandparents are pushing the kids towards screens and devices. Addiction to screens and devices is no less than addiction to drugs. Are we pushing our young children towards a lethal addiction; that would harm them now and in years to come? *Are we harming our children by over exposing them to technology during their most impressionable years?* We may not see the adverse impact of devices and screens today, but it will become apparent when history of our times is written. Our children and grandchildren are our most precious possessions; let us keep an open mind and protect them.

16

Do We Live by
Choice or by Chance?

*"Sir, the paralysis is in my legs I will
never, ever, let it get to my head."*

The road of life has many bends, and it depends on us how
we negotiate them. When I passed out of St Xavier's'
School, Patna, I got admission to the pre-medical course in
Patna Medical College, and to the National Defence
Academy, Khadakvasla, Pune. I chose to join the National
Defence Academy. In 1962, life in the National Defence
Academy was tough, very tough. The day started with early
morning PT, riding, drill, and weapon training, followed by
academics; the afternoon was devoted to sporting activities
including swimming; and study periods were scheduled for
the evening. Ragging was very prevalent in those days and,
it was quite natural for a sixteen year old boy to feel
depressed, at times. A friend of mine, Dinkar (name
changed), was always happy; and one day I had to ask him,
"Dinkar how is it you are always happy?". He replied,
"Every morning when I wake up, I promise myself that I
will be happy. So, whenever I feel depressed, I remind
myself of my promise." We completed our three year
training in National Defence Academy, Pune, followed by
another one year in the Indian Military Academy at
Dehradun; and subsequently, we went our separate ways.

Dinkar joined the Infantry, and I the Armoured Corps. After a few years I heard that Dinkar had been critically injured in counter insurgency operations, and was fighting a life and death battle.

Thirty years later, while playing a game of golf at the Army Golf Course, in Jallandhar, I thought I saw Dinkar in the adjacent fairway. I walked up to him, and he recognized me immediately. That evening we had a reunion, a grand reunion, just Dinkar and me. After a few drinks I asked him "Dinkar, how did you overcome being critically wounded and live?" He said, "You remember how in the National Defence Academy days, I used to tell myself every day, that I must be happy? I kept telling myself that I have to live, before I lost consciousness. Well, here I am this evening having my fourth drink with you!" In the National Defence Academy Dinkar took the choice to be happy and on that fateful day Dinkar took the choice to live. Dinkar lived his life by choice.

After retirement I took to a lot of travelling. On one such trip, I was spending a few hours at the Changi airport Singapore, awaiting the next flight. In the lounge, next to me was a group of five young people probably in their thirties, also awaiting a connecting flight. They were having a hilarious time. The leader was a handsome, smart, young man in a wheelchair, paralyzed below the waist. I walked up to him and after a few pleasantries told him, that he seemed remarkably happy. He looked me in the eye and said, *"Sir, the paralysis is in my legs I will never, ever, let it get to my head."* He had decided to live by choice.

Having taken to public speaking I was doing a short course on communication skills. In my class was a eighty four year old lady, and once while talking to her, I asked her why she was doing the course. At first she joked, that it was to meet a nice young man, get married, and have grandchildren! Then on a more serious note, she replied, "we spend our entire lives communicating. As children we communicate with our parents, siblings, teachers, friends; on growing up communication continues with our spouse, children, colleagues. From birth to death, communication forms a very important part of our lives. So now that I have time, I decided, why not learn to communicate better?" She had taken the choice to keep improving and making a better edition of herself, impervious to age!

Why is it some of us are born blind, some so talented that they become world famous, some tall and handsome, some beautiful. Is this not also by chance? But we still definitely have a choice. The young man at Changi airport had taken the choice to be happy. Helen Keller became blind at a young age, yet her work made her immortal. She had taken her choice of not letting her blindness come in the way of her life. In the Mahabharat the Pandava brothers took the choice to follow the course of dharma (righteousness), while Duryodhana chose the path of adharma (unrighteousness).

Each one of us has one life to live. We all want to be successful, wealthy, healthy, and happy. God has given us life that is like an orchestra; it is up to each one of us, which instrument we pick up, and how we play it. I took the choice to join the army, and serve my country. Dinkar when critically wounded took the choice to live. Helen Keller though blind, chose to live her life to the full.

Subaltern Days

Anybody can make himself uncomfortable; it requires an intelligent man to make himself comfortable.

Being a subaltern is unique; one not to be seen or heard, one simply exists. Shortly after joining the 16 Light Cavalry, I had to set up a field camp, so that some top brass could partridge shoot by early next morning. During dinner that night in the camp mess, the Brigade Commander (Buch) gave a discourse on the duties of a regimental quarter master to the other brass. As the camp in-charge I was the only officer from the Regiment present and on listening watch.

A few months later during the Administrative Inspection, I found myself officiating as the Quartermaster, and awaiting arrival of the Brigade Commander in the Quartermaster's store. The first salvo that was fired at me was, "what are the duties of a Quartermaster?" I repeated verbatim his discourse at the camp. With a look of amazement he asked me where I had learnt all this. I promptly replied that my Commanding Officer Col Harbans Singh had taught me all this. Now it was the Commanding Officer's turn to look bewildered. Thereafter, I was his blue eyed boy, and could do no wrong!

It was the formation test exercise. My Centurion tank was positioned in a perfect 'hull-down' position in the blistering summer sun of Punjab. The wireless set crackled and my Squadron Commander (Maj Surendra Nath) said "Good position, however there is an equally good position fifty yards from where you are under a shady tree. *Anybody can make himself uncomfortable, it requires an intelligent man to make himself comfortable"*. I heed his advice till this day.

A dozen of us subalterns were lined up for the retention examination. I was the first to go for the weapon training practical. After the practical test, on my way back I exchanged some pleasantries with my colleagues awaiting their turn. Next morning I was in the Second-in-Command's office (then Maj Krishnamurthi), vehemently denying that I had given out questions. I was let off after being told that if I was in a toddy shop, nobody would believe that I was having milk!

After two years of existence as a "Mr" our witty Second-in-Command (Morris) was heard telling the Brigade Major (Maj Subia) on telephone that "Mr Chakravarti is no more", and followed a long, very long pause, "He has become a Captain!!" My happy, carefree days of being a subaltern were over.

Then and Now

Where the world will be when our grandchildren reach our age, only time will tell.

It was my school holidays and I as a nine year old boy had gone to visit my my Dadu (maternal grandfather) and Didu (maternal grandmother) who lived in Berhampur 600 km, away from Kolkata. Every morning at 6 AM my Choto Mama (younger uncle), who was preparing for the Joint Services Wing examination for entry to the National Defence Academy, took me to the Ganges riverside. I saw many men jogging on the banks or swimming in the river, all of whom were well built, with V shaped bodies. Choto Mama and I after jogging in the fresh air, recited the Gayatri Mantra (prayer) on the bank of the Ganga, and went home for a cold-water bath, after applying coconut or mustard oil on the body and hair. This was followed by a hearty breakfast of doi chirda (curd and flattened rice), aloo luchi (aloo puri) or the like. Then off to school or work on foot or by cycle, very few families owned cars. In those days everyone lived in a big joint family. The houses were huge sprawling bungalows, with invariably a big courtyard in the centre. It was the meeting place where family members congregated to sit together and chat, as and when they had free time. Each family had six or more children.

The women of the house looked after the children, walked them down to school, and on the way back did the shopping, besides the cooking and household work. There were no gyms, walking/jogging tracks. Each meal was a hearty meal and the word dieting was unheard of, definitely no keto and vegan meals. Yet it was almost a rarity to spot an obese person.

Beauty products were non-existent. No creams, moisturizers, lotions, anti-wrinkle creams, perfumes with exotic names and brands. Our ladies applied 'malai' (meegada in English) and 'haldi' (turmeric) on their face and body. Pimples and rashes were unheard of; the skin was smooth, flawless, and glowing. From their late teens the girls wore saris which covered their bodies elegantly. Slim narrow waistlines and long flowing hair, growing with grace and beauty into womanhood. Classical and semi-classical music and dance were learnt by all. Marriages were arranged early by parents. Men were the bread earners, women raised children, and were the home makers. Joint families were cardinal to sharing each other's company, joy, happiness and sorrow. Children and adults were taught by the elders to give respect and reverence to seniors. Grandparents pursued activities of their choice, and found joy and pleasure in playing with the grandchildren when they wished to.

Since then, seven decades of my life have gone by and everything has changed. The respectful pranam (touching the feet) has been replaced with a casual 'hi', and the joyous joint families with nuclear families. The modest graceful saris have been replaced by daring, seductive clothing; the learning of classical dances has given way to lesser dance forms. Late marriages, late children, working parents, grandparents and maids bringing up the children are the norm of the day. Live in partners are common, and thought of as a preferred way of life. Women are economically independent. The only child syndrome is replacing larger families. More and more children are living abroad. Senior citizens homes are replacing joint families, where old parents go to spend their remaining days.

With time change is inevitable. Some changes are for the better and some for the worse. Adjustment is essential for the older generation. A new era has taken over, ushered in by Science and Technology; with instant communication converting the world into a global village. The elderly have to keep up with computer skills, to meet their day to day needs. Knowledge of online payment of bills, ordering of commodities, internet banking, surfing, video communication with children and grandchildren, have become essential to living. An era when material success is valued beyond human relationships. Wealth decides your status and success story; principles, values and ethics are fast diminishing. With every decade the world takes on a different shade and colour. Whether the world is changing for the better or worse is judged by each one of us, from our own perspective of life. In certain aspects, the changes are for the better, and in some, for the worse. ***Where the world will be when our grandchildren reach our age, only time will tell.*** One can only hope that they live in a better world. Will our wishes come true?

Be a Winner

The winners are those who do something about their dreams.

"Winner" is a fashionable word I often hear when interacting with the corporate world. It is a label for those going places in the corporate ladder. To me the word "Winner" brings to mind Capt JK Sengupta, of the 16 Light Cavalry, popularly known as "Jojo". A gold medallist from National Defence Academy, Sword of honour recipient from Indian Military Academy and the Silver Tank awardee from the Armoured Corps Centre and School. Jojo tragically lost his eyesight in the 1965 Indo-Pak War and was boarded out of service. After the war, I met Jojo in 1970 in Patiala. We had finished dinner in the Officers Mess, when I received a call from the Commanding Officer that as Adjutant, I was required to personally deliver a document to the Divisional Headquarter at Ambala that very night. On hearing this, Jojo insisted that he accompany me, as it meant driving throughout the night. We next met in 1980 at Jodhpur during the Regimental Day Celebrations. The Inter-Squadron 400 metres relay was on. The one cheering the loudest was Jojo; he had lost his eyesight but not his spirits. The 'Jojos' of the world with their positive attitude and dreams are the true winners in life.

A positive attitude and mental picture takes us from one accomplishment to another. When we have a dream, a mental picture, we are not just spectators. We are taking part in shaping the purpose and meaning of our lives. Of course, there is a big difference between those who dream and those who make their dreams come true. ***The winners are those who do something about their dreams.*** Attitude is the magic word which makes us do something about our dreams. Attitude is what makes people winners. They may have gone through the hardships and downtimes, yet their attitude keeps returning them to the top. Attitude is what helps us to realize our dreams by looking at the world through positive expectations and beliefs. Jojo was a true model of all these attributes put into one. We all feel very proud that a man like Jojo served in 16 Light Cavalry and fought a war.

Jojo used to come to Bangalore often to see his daughter, and meet his good friend Gen Natrajan, who is also settled in Bangalore. On those occasions I had the proud opportunity to meet him. It is rare to come across a man of his stature.

The difference between a winner and a loser in life is the hardening of negative attitudes. Losers are those who for years have been warehousing old hates, expectations of failures, fears, remorse, guilt, revenge and so on.

The longer I live, the more I realize the impact of dreams and attitudes on life. Attitude is more than facts. It is more important than education. money, talent, skill, and appearance. It makes us winners or losers in life. No matter what our age is, no matter what our past has been, our future is spotless. We can begin pursuing our dreams, right from today. We can be winners. We can try and emulate Jojo as a homage to him.

The Goal

My heart was brimming with joy, all
because of a cancelled goal.

Milkha Singh, the flying Sikh from the Services, is a name in all households. Personnel of the armed forces, and their wives, have excelled in all sports and games, at the international events. Deepa Malik, an army officer's wife, was the first Indian woman to win a silver medal in shot put, in the summer Paralympic games of 2016. Sports play a significant role in the armed forces, and for a very good reason. It instills character in a person; and it is character which inspires a soldier to face bullets and defend his country.

Regiments which have a cherished history are very proud of their prowess in sports. My regiment the 16 Light Cavalry, and the 5 Mechanized Infantry, both formed part of the same armoured brigade. Both regiments fiercely proud of their football reputation were the finalists of the brigade football tournament. It would be a do or die, high voltage game. And, of course, only one could win! Both regiments started their preparations in real earnest. Players were excused from all duties so that they could spend all their time training in football. Coaches were brought from the Regimental Centre. Extra diet of unlimited eggs and milk was authorized for each player. Our officer's mess cook was our ace left winger. Our wives volunteered to cook for the bachelors so that Cook Raju was free to practice. Officers, men and ladies discussed the forthcoming football match all day long. Cheering teams were formed, cheer leaders were nominated, and cheer slogans were thought of and practiced. Every one offered advice on strategy to be adopted. Spies were sent to discreetly study the game of the opposing team. New outfits were made for the team. The ladies decided to wear a sari with regimental colours and the order was promptly placed by the Risaldar Major. As the day of reckoning approached the tension kept rising and became unbearable. Children were excited and would not go to school on the day of the match. As the Commanding Officer, I took a special Sainik Sammelan(durbar) to motivate the players.

Finally, it was the day of the match; we woke up to a bright sunny glorious morning. The match was scheduled at 4 PM in the evening at Kapurthala, where the 5 Mechanized Infantry were located. It was a distance of 135 km from Amritsar where we were stationed. Except for those on essential duties, all others would go. Three-ton vehicles were marshaled for the men. A separate three ton was organized for the cheering party with the drums. The officers, wives and children would go in jeeps and jongas; the families of the men in one-ton vehicles. Before the convoy moved from the regimental lines, the regiment priest offered prayers.We arrived well in time. It was a blistering hot afternoon in the summer of Punjab. The stadium was jam packed with spectators; the entire brigade was there to witness this much trumpeted match, whose reputation had preceded it. The crowd was no less than a Mohan Bagan versus East Bengal club match.

The captains went up for the toss. We lost the toss and were at a disadvantage playing with the sun in our eyes. The teams entered and players took up their positions. The game started and from the very first minute both teams showed their 'josh'(enthusiasm). The 5 Mechanized Infantry had a very good team with each player playing a superb game. For the first half the ball was mostly in our half. Our goal keeper did some miraculous saves. Till half time the game was scoreless. During the fifteen minutes interval I walked up to the players. I told them that the game was very much open till the last minute, till the very end. Our players should continue with their efforts and play a fair game without fouling. The sportsman spirit was important and should prevail, the result was a bonus. In the second half the game was evenly matched. Till the fortieth minute of the second half, there was no score. Thereafter within seconds, Raju the cook got a good pass, he ran with the ball along the left flank, he seemed faster than Usain Bolt, and then put in a brilliant shot. Hurray, it was a goal! The drums and cheering were deafening.

In the midst of the cheering our team captain walked up to the referee and was seen talking. He had just informed the referee that the goal was an off side by his player. The referee signaled cancellation of the goal due to being off side. Consternation was written all over the faces of 16 Cavalry ranks. Suddenly there was an eerie silence. What had our team Captain done?! Why, why, why? Just three minutes were now left for the game to end in a draw. Just then in a lightening move, our centre forward appeared as if from nowhere with the ball, and with an unbelievable dribble, shot the ball into the goal! 16 Cavalry had won the match 1-0!!

The whole of 16 Light Cavalry was ecstatic with joy at winning the match. I realized at that moment that I had achieved my aim as a Commanding Officer of having instilled sterling character qualities in the ranks. Winning or losing was not of primary importance. I had done my job well. A regiment with character would always perform well in war and that was the dream of every Commanding Officer. *My heart was brimming with joy, all because of a cancelled goal.*

The Changing Face of Generations

*Is it because we have convinced
ourselves that our only purpose of
living now is for our children?*

My mind goes back to the evening I went to visit an eighty five year old gentlemen in an old age home in Bangalore. Though now old and infirm, he was very erudite and a highly educated man, who had held high positions in office. He and his equally erudite wife lived in the flat above mine. I first met them after retirement when I came to settle down in Sena Vihar Bangalore. At that time, he was 75 years old. I always liked to hear his well-informed views on all matters; be it history, technology, mythology or any other subject. We would meet every morning during walks. On chilly winter mornings, he invariably admonished my wife, for not protecting her head from the cold! They had two daughters settled in USA; both very fine ladies, who visited their parents occasionally, at their convenience. As their parents grew older, they tried to persuade their parents to live with them abroad. The old couple insisted they would live in their own country, in their own flat, amidst their known environment, and live their lives on their own terms, independently! The girls could return if they so wished.

As the years progressed, the wife died and six months later, the aged man's health deteriorated. His daughters came to take him with them. He insisted on staying in Bangalore, and opted to being shifted to an old age home. Four months later he died. Being very fond of him I visited him several times. This suffering, fragile old man put up a brave, cheerful front till the very last day. His mind was crystal clear, and he discussed the tank battles of the Second World War till his last day. His sunset years made a lasting impression on my mind, and made me ponder over the future which awaits us.

The very concept of the modern old age home is comparatively new to India. It is not the old age home of yester years which paints a dismal picture of dilapidated buildings, where the unwanted destitute were dumped. The old age homes of today are posh colonies with clubs, malls, medical centers and all the modern facilities. All your needs like housekeeping, cooking, shopping, medical, maintenance and repair of your home are attended to. At the same time, you stay in the ambience of your own country, meet your children when they come to visit you, or you go on a holiday to see them. In India, parents in their old age are expected to stay with their children. Staying away is frowned upon. Yet you find more and people opting for comfortable old age homes.

Why are old age homes mushrooming in India, is it because the joint family system has broken up? Or can we attribute it to the global village with many of our children working and settled abroad? Obviously, it is not possible to look after the daily requirements of aging parents, from far away or distant places. Children try to persuade parents to come and live with them. Are the parents willing to give up their homes, friends, and the environment, where they have spent many long years? The park where all the oldies meet every morning for a constitutional walk, followed by a cup of hot tea, welcomed warmly by the chaiwallah(tea seller), who has seen them for so many years. The long exuberant conversations and the recollecting incidents of the yesteryear! The weekly golf fourballs in a nearby golf course, the same jokes being repeated during every game, and the joyful back slapping when a golfer scores a par! The bonhomie, brotherhood, and the hearty breakfast at the club house. The glass of whisky in the evenings, to go over every stroke, each one of us played that morning. Our wives playfully scolding us while preparing a pot luck dinner for us. Our homes, our friends, our time, our lives to live the way we want to, without any restrictions placed on us.

The golfers of Sena Vihar at a cocktail

The ladies Mahjong and the tea parties during the games. Exchanging notes about children and grandchildren, enthusiastically celebrating birthdays, anniversaries. The wholehearted mega celebrations of golden jubilee anniversaries and landmark birthdays. The regular colony movies, tombola, and Speakers Forum meets, with the added pleasure of meeting all our colony friends and snacks replacing dinner. The day long Diwali melas, the ending highlight being the lucky draw. *Thirty* draws to be picked out. Who will be the lucky ones? The anticipation, excitement, and expectation on every face; as each name is announced the cheering reaching a crescendo, and the sigh of disappointment when it is not! The fun and celebrations at the New Year Eve functions. The feeling of warmth and belonging to your own colony, and being amongst your friends. Oh, to leave all this behind, and go to an alien land?

Is this the dilemma that many an elderly person has to face? Whether to go and live with their children abroad, leaving homes and belonging, to which they have become attached, over the past so many years. The favorite rocking chair, the curios your wife and you bought from the places you visited in India and abroad, and lovingly preserved for all these years. The many memories you shared, for each curio, each painting. Leave behind your friends of over five decades. And, in a way leave behind your lives, knowing that the children have their own lives to live; and much as they love you, have very little time for you, from their busy schedule. To adopt to the routine of another home, where timings are laid down, rather than spend the twilight years of your life, in your own home. The savings you have so painstakingly collected, and the pension you get, makes it possible to live in a lavish, princely manner in your own country; but loses value when compared to the hard currency of advanced countries. In a way, it is a loss of your independence, and the beginning of becoming dependents. Is it because it is easier to be do-gooders and succumb to the demands of our children? Is it because we begin to lose trust in our own capabilities, decisions, and begin to believe that the children know best? Is it because of the misplaced notion that being good parents means helping the children? Helping in household work, and bringing up our grandchildren; while the children earn double income salaries in foreign lands, where domestic help is very difficult to employ. *Is it because we have convinced ourselves that our only purpose of living now is for our children?*

We love our children, and want to be with them. We certainly want to help our children. At the same time, we deserve to live our lives the way it makes us happy. It is certainly unfair to expect the children to relocate to be close to us. In a like manner, the parents too, have a right to their own lives. Is this the dilemma which confronts many of us? What is the remedy? Are modern old age homes the answer? No worries about maids, cooks, our medical needs. Is it the best of both worlds? Enabling us to lead our own lives amongst our friends, having our club life, all the things we do, and yet, be with the children whenever we want. Has this dilemma been brought about by the changing face of generations?

Companion

We had a joyous evening and that is when my friendship with my companion started.

Five decades ago, nobody had heard of the internet and mobiles; communication was by way of letters and land line telephone, even subscriber trunk dialing had not been introduced. Out station calls had to booked with the operator and took hours sometimes days to come through. It was in the month of April 1972 that I had written a letter to a wonderful girl, proposing that we become life partners. A few weeks later on a bright, cheerful April afternoon I received a call from her, which became the stepping stone to spending our life together. April became my favorite month.

That evening I, with my companion, went to a friend's house to celebrate. *We had a joyous evening and that is when my friendship with my companion started.* We got married in August in the far away town of Kotagiri, tucked into the beautiful blue mountains of the Nilgiris. My companion came all the way with me to Kotagiri; and returned with me and my new bride to Ahmednagar, where I was posted as a young captain. It was a nice quiet station with lots of time after office hours and a salubrious climate, ideally meant for newly weds.

So, many an evening was spent sitting in the spacious front verandah, with my wife and my companion. We savored the delicious snacks made by John the Chinaman, who ran a Chinese cafeteria in the Officers' Institute. It was invariably followed by a sumptuous dinner. As the years went by, I got posted from one station to another. Work pressure increased, and the responsibilities at home got more and more; with bringing up a child, parents aging, fulfilling official and social commitments. Leisurely evenings became far and few, when my wife and I could sit together with my companion.

As time went by, occasionally some other companion was brought, but the evening passed without a feeling of satisfaction. It never was the same, without my faithful companion. On all our celebrations, be they birthdays, anniversaries, New Year's eve, and promotions, the evenings just had to be together. I could not imagine life, without my companion. Then came Covid -19, and with it the seemingly interminable lockdowns. Though a good deal of time has passed since then, I have not spent a single evening with my companion! Travel abroad has been restricted, and with it the non-availability, and opportunity to be with my companion.

On an evening, confined to my house due to the Covid-19 lockdown, I was missing my companion. I remembered all the good times we have had since our first meeting that April, almost fifty years ago. The day, when I went to my friend's house in Ahmednagar, to celebrate the good news of my engagement, and took my companion along! It was then, that with a sense of shock, I realized that I could not remember my companion's name. I did not enjoy my dinner, and had a restless night. Tossing and turning, feeling guilty, and like a traitor. How could I ever forget my companion's name?

Next morning while having my tea, the name came back in a flash! Oh, what a sense of relief!! Then and there, I told my wife, that the evening would be spent like old times, she, I and my companion. It was a grand reunion, this time with delicious snacks from Mary's Gazebo café, the restaurant in our colony.

Meet Chivas Regal, my companion of the past fifty years.

Beta Naam Karega

The father who once said, "Mera beta naam karega", was now fervently chanting, 'Mera beta kaam karega'.

Pune 1954, I am in class four of Bishop Cotton School. I have come accompanied by my parents to attend the annual prize distribution for meritorious performance in academics and sports. One cup in sports and two books in academics are awarded to me. Refreshments are served after the prize distribution. The principal and teachers move around and talk to the parents, with a congratulatory word to some, and cautionary advice to others. My parents are pleased but feel somewhat deflated because their best friend's son, also in my class, has won more prizes than me. On reaching home I am given a pat on the back, but in the same breath told, that I must work harder, so that next time I win more prizes than Rahul, their best friend's son.

On the birth of a child, every father firmly believes, wishes, and announces that his child will bring name and fame to himself and his parents. The unforgettable lines from the yesteryear song "papa kehte hain beta naam karega", resonate perfectly with this sentiment. Parents take it upon themselves to live their dreams through their children. I was no different and did the same, except, in my case it was my 'beti'(daughter). Now, in my silver years as a grandfather, I sit back and see the world through clearer lenses. The interpretation, and perspective of achievements, and 'naam' (name or fame) differs from generation to generation.

As a child I heard with reverence the names of Bhagat Singh and Udham Singh, the socialist revolutionaries and freedom fighters. Their indomitable stand against the British, going to the gallows with a smile on their lips, and singing 'Vande matram' made them hallowed household names that will survive the test of time. For the British they were infamous, whereas for every Indian they are famous, immortal heroes of our Independence movement, dying as they did for our country. The names of Rani Lakshmibai, Bikaji Rustom Cama, Sarojini Naidu, Sardar Vallabhai Patel, Babasaheb Ambedkar and Subhash Chandra Bose are immortalized by their valiant struggle for the freedom of India.

Today, the thousands of our soldiers at the borders, protect the integrity of our mother land and are fully prepared for the supreme sacrifice of their lives. Many of them have done heroic feats been martyred, awarded the nation's highest gallantry award the Param Vir Chakra. Immortalized and forever connected with the Indo-Pakistan Wars, are Maj Adi Tarapore (1965) Maj Somnath Sharma(1947), Arun Khetrapal (1971) and Capt Vikram Batra(1999) 'the dil mange more', hero of Kargil. One cannot discuss the 1962 Indo-China War without remembering the astounding bravery of Maj Dhan Singh Thapa in 1962. Will they become by words for bravery and courage in every Indian home, a hundred years from now, like Bhagat Singh?

After Independence our country had netas(leaders) of impeccable character, integrity and honesty. They joined politics to serve the nation. Lal Bahadur Shastri, Atal Bihari Vajpayee, and others left a stamp in politics as netas and have acquired name and fame. Today people join politics for money, power and perks. Has the concept of 'naam' changed?

Playing in the Indian cricket team makes one rich and legendary. The film stars are bold, beautiful, rich and famous, though in the days of yore joining the film world was frowned upon. The television screens of national channels went berserk and ramped up the suicide case of the actor Sushant Singh Rajput, allegedly for increasing their name and fame. Has the interpretation of making a 'naam' changed?

The year was 1960, the place Jallandhar, a group of five boys, all 16 and 17 years old, were on holiday with their parents. We had just appeared for Senior Cambridge examination, and were awaiting the results. All of us were good students from good institutions like the Doon School in Dehradun, the Mayo College in Ajmer, and St. Xavier's High School in Patna. The whole big world seemed to be at our feet, waiting to welcome us into the fold. Now, the first big important step had to be taken; the careful selection of a profession. What were we looking for? An easy life, with comfort, money, name and fame? Some of us had already obtained admission to premier medical and engineering colleges. The desire to protect and defend our territorial borders attracted us to the armed forces. We considered it a noble profession. Our fathers were happy with our choice. It fulfilled their wish of 'beta naam karega'. Four of us friends decided to join the army. At that time army was considered a good career. It was a noble profession, and name and fame went with it. Today, rather unfortunately, the army is considered a less than favorite choice.

Thirty two years later in 1992 my daughter had appeared for the CBSE examination and was waiting with her friends, both girls and boys for the results. Again, from good schools, and good students. The parents wish of 'beta/beti mera naam karega', had not changed from my student days This time the criteria for most of the children and parents was the earning capacity of the profession. Money equaled 'naam', and consequently, the perception of 'naam' had undergone a sea change!

I was posted in Mumbai as the Deputy General Officer Commanding an army formation. By virtue of my designation, I was invited to a corporate dinner with the top head honchos of big business houses. All their children were perusing their under graduation or post graduation abroad, generally not on merit but on scholarships borne by their fathers. The more expensive the school, the more pride the father evinced that his beta had 'naam'. Both father and son lived under illusions, powered by money. They enjoyed exotic holidays during vacations, first class air travel, the best living accommodation, expensive cars, clothes, the best of what the world could offer. After completing their studies many of the children refused to take up jobs. After all, why should they work, when all their needs were being met by their families. The father manipulated one job after another for the children, but after a brief spell they left the job. The psychiatrists were of the opinion it was a disease that is slowly increasing in many parts of the world, amongst the children of the super rich parents. ***The father who once said, "Mera beta naam karega" was now fervently chanting ' Mera beta kaam karega'.***

Today name and fame is synonymous with money and power, both of which fan the ego and pride, and become the root cause of all evil. Many of us spend the better part of our lives chasing money and power, which gives us in return greed, jealousy, vengeance, the perfect recipe for unhappiness. At the later stages of our life, we realize with deep regret that we have missed the mission of life. Life is meant to serve humanity, give more and receive less, sacrifice and share. Achieve happiness, love, and light. We spend our life chasing mirages. We forget the very purpose of life. We forget the Biblical quote which says "for dust thou art and unto dust shalt return".

I Married a 'Civilian'

I was summoned and told that being newly married, I was permitted to leave a party whenever I desired, for the next six months.

On a refreshing April morning in 1972, I was gallivanting in Connaught Place, New Delhi, a young, carefree cavalier, breaking journey for two days on my way back from annual leave. Little did I know that on that red letter day, I would be meeting the charming young lady with whom I was to spend the rest of my life.

We got married at Kotagiri, a scenic small town in the blue mountains of the Nilgiris. After a week, I, a die-hard soldier from the National Defence Academy, accompanied by my new bride, who had absolutely no connection with the army, reached Ahmednagar. We were received by my Regimental Officer, who in his shiny black new fiat car, drove us to our temporary quarters, a four room hutment with one of rooms having no roof! My wife after inspecting the hutment, nonchalantly commented that this would do for the staff, and now we should drive to our residence. Sensing trouble, I was taken aside by my friend, handed the keys of the car, and told to go on a holiday for a week to Ajanta and Ellora, while he would see what could be done to the hutment.

After some time, just when I felt content that my wife was acclimatised to the army environment and my troubles were over, we were required to attend a function at the Officers' Institute. All was well till dinner was over and the Commandant, a Maha Vir Chakra awardee, a long-time widower and a person fond of his drinks, decided to enjoy a few more pegs. My 'civilian' wife walked up to the Commandant, and in all sincerity queried why others could not leave while he enjoyed his drinks? The grand old man bellowed with laughter, *I was summoned and told that being newly married, I was permitted to leave a party whenever I desired, for the next six months.*

A few months later, I proceeded to Mhow in Madhya Pradesh to attend the Junior Command Course, and my wife accompanied me since families were permitted. On the course, there were strict instructions that the student officers were not to be informed of their grading. More

45

than the officers, the wives were keen that, their husbands do well. During the mid-term social evening, I overheard my dear wife loudly announcing that I was coming third on course. There was consternation all around as the Commandant was standing close by. The Commandant who was a terror, expressed his desire to meet the young lady. My wife who by nature was never awed by any situation was escorted to the Commandant, and on being asked how she knew her husband was coming third, confidently declared that since all the other wives were saying that their husbands were coming first or second, so I must be third!

After taking over a brigade, I took my wife in the staff car flying my flag, my chest filled with pride. She looked at me and asked innocently "why are you flying this flag? My father always flew the National flag. I could not but laugh at my civilian wife. You see, I had married an ambassador's daughter.

During all the married years when I was in uniform, she remained fiercely independent, honest, frank, and was never impressed or awed by rank or position. On most occasions, senior officers appreciated her attitude, and she endeared herself to most of them, who remember her fondly, and many, still keep in touch with her.

Years went by, and while my colleagues' wives became more and more engrossed in their husbands' promotions and careers, my wife remained a delightfully refreshing civilian, happy and content with her family, hobbies and job.

Now we live in a retired officers' colony, where all the name boards boldly display ranks and decorations. Our name board reads 'Chaks and Nanu' just as we are known amongst our friends. Thank God for that April day when I met my 'civilian' wife!

Politics and the Common Man

This is the age of brand names, brand slogans and brand strategies. "Amul: The Taste of India" and, "Hyundai: Take Home a Relationship." Advertising corporates and gurus work full time on it. Models and media make a fortune in this age of brands by show casing brands and products. Not to be left behind, politicians have on their pay roll the best brains to ramp up their own and the party's image; and lower the opposition leaders and party's image with the use of brand names and slogans.

Tuesdays are my golfing days. On one Tuesday my golfing four ball said we should not go for golf as 'Raga' would be in town, and traffic jams are likely. The day after I was informed that 'Pappu' had left, and it was safe to go for golf. Not being abreast of matters political, I was surprised how 'Raga' had come and 'Pappu' was going. A few days later my wife asked me not to go to town as our PM Namo was here to address a rally, and discovered, I had no idea that we had a new PM! The highlight of the month was my golf at a high-end golf course situated in a resort on the outskirts of Bangalore. You can imagine my disappointment when I was told that, 'Yadu' with hundred others were holed up in the resort. Being a golfer, I knew that the ball was lined up for a putt and on a par three you teed off hoping for a hole in one. But how could hundred people be holed up? I had heard of Tiger Wood, Anirban Lahiri and other well-known golfers but who was this 'Yadu'?

One of the criteria by which a Neta's speech is judged is the number of slogans given out. As a nation we are very vocal. When we speak in one block, we can be heard two blocks away. You can imagine the jubilation of the masses on hearing the slogan "vocal for local"? Being a staunch patriot the next time I went to a shop and was about to ask in a loud voice for a local product, I stopped short, wondering whether "Made in India" or "Made by India" would be correct. Slogans often have a reverse effect. For many years I have been hearing the slogans "garibi hatao"; but garibi (poverty) refuses to budge. I had heard with a lot of hope "jai kisan, jai jawan". Many years have gone past, but the fate of the kisan (farmer) and jawan (soldier) have not changed. Was the exodus of migrants to their villages brought about by "Ghar Wapsi"? Being a boxer I knew what a knockout punch was but did not know that knock out slogans were prepared for the opposition, "gali, gali, men shor hai, XXX chor hai"

Soft skill trainers have a flourishing business. Great emphasis is laid on body language. Top netas (leaders) are taught to make full use of the soft touch skill of the embrace. During the frequent foreign trips of our netas to other countries to further diplomatic relations; the success of a trip is determined from the number of 'jhapis'(hugs). Our netas excel in this! It appears, Mr Corona objected to these frequent 'jhapis', and brought along the idea of the corona virus. Now there are no handshakes, jhapis or pappies (kisses). It is once more, either the good old culture of namaste, or the new normal of touching elbows.

Staying for too long in one party results in boredom and familiarity. Therefore, it is quite natural for several members of one party, to take a stroll across the floor to the new environment of the other party. This merely results in a change of government. The media gets into a tizzy on prime time, but the public remain calm, as it makes little difference which party comes, or which goes.

At the end of the day, one is tired and dreary. That is when our understanding media, put up some of the best comedy shows on national television. During the panel discussions, especially chosen comedians participate as party spokespersons. The day ends on a happy note, and we look forward to more fun and games, on the next day, thanks to our politics and politicians. God bless our politics and politicians!

Are Meetings Predestined?

It was the winter of 1965 in the city of Kanpur in Uttar Pradesh where winters are known for being severe. On a cold foggy morning in December an elderly lady, about fifty-five years old was standing at the gate of her bungalow, with a utensil in her hand waiting for the milkman to arrive. To her surprise, a poor woman in her twenties fell at her feet. She was clad in a white sari and blouse carrying a baby girl, a few months old. She begged her in Bengali to be given shelter and food. She had come from Kolkata with her husband; a blacksmith who had been promised a job. Her husband had died a few days ago in an unfortunate road accident. She did not have a family, and her husband's family would not take her back. Both the young woman and her baby had not eaten since then, and had no shelter. She was destitute, and begged to be taken as a domestic help.

It so happened at that time, the lady of the house needed someone to help with the house work. On an impulse, she took the woman and her baby in. Just she and her husband were staying by themselves, after he had retired. Her four children, two sons and two daughters were well placed in life and living far away. The few months old baby girl was brought up in the same way as her four children. The girl after completing Master's was married to a boy from a poor family holding a grade one government job. Today, forty years later the destitute girl has two teenage children, a boy and a girl, a good husband, house and a car. From a destitute baby she lives now in a comfortable position. Was it all because of a predestined chance meeting?

October of 1965, Military Hospital at Jammu. The Indo Pak war was just over, and the hospital was overflowing with casualties. Amongst the wounded was a handsome young captain from the Maratha Light Infantry, whose right leg had been amputated from above the knee. Patriotic emotions were running high amongst the people. Young men and women from colleges and various institutions were visiting the wounded with goodies and kind words. Having just lost a leg the young captain was not very inclined to talk. However, there was a young lady who used to come to the ward at five in the evening, every day. The captain looked forward to her visit. There was something that set her apart from the others. Well educated, knowledgeable, positive, and sincere with several interests and hobbies. Her father was also a war wounded. With each day, their fondness for each other grew, and over time the two of them decided to get married. Throughout their married life they have remained a made for each other couple. The young captain, despite the handicap of his disability, rose to a very high rank. A chance meeting at a hospital bed, had led to a life-long bonding! Are meetings predestined?

On retiring twenty years ago I settled in colony in Bangalore. One evening during my evening walk I saw an old lady also on a walk. I walked across the road and wished her. Instinctively her face broke into a smile and she addressed me as "twinkle eyes". From that day onwards, we met every evening. I was twinkle eyes to her and she was "madam" to me. During our daily chats I learnt from her the true value of humility, of not complaining of problems, and appreciating all that one had! I learnt the art of listening, and my life became so much more meaningful. A chance meeting had also changed my life!

Gadgor Day When
I Was Ten Years Old

by Bashuli Sane

It meant two days of feasting, fun,
skipping school, and no study.

"Gadgor Day" came every year on the 8th of September. It was the Battle Honours Day of my father's regiment earned during the 1965 war. My friend Roopali and I looked forward to it eagerly. ***It meant two days of feasting, fun,***

skipping school, and no study. The Pagal Gymkhana where we kids vied with each other to claim the passenger seat with Pushkar uncle in the cycle rickshaw race. He always won the race and the lucky passenger also got a prize. In the fancy dress the same beggar man year after year, was a great source of amusement. The joy ride for us kids in a train towed by a jeep with a number of attached trolleys was a highlight. Doraiswamy bhaiya was always in charge of us kids. The high tea which followed, had us kids rushing to the cake to eat only the icing. In the evening, there was the Barakhana or grand, dinner with a separate enclosure for each squadron. We children gleefully visited each squadron enclosure and ate to our heart's content! The entertainment programme had the inevitable tiger dance. The next day pin drop silence at the memorial parade being broken by Aditya Yadav's loud whisper "mama mujhe bhook laga" (Ma, I am hungry).

The closing of Gadgor Day was marked by a grand dinner in the officers' mess. Kids were huddled into one room and supplied with a continuous supply of Coca Cola and snacks. Dinner was brought in early for us and the 'bacha uncles', Adil, Sumer, Soumitra, Anand and Deepak always dropped in for a bite. The finale of Gadgor Day was when Baba brought home the photographs. I grabbed the ones where I featured and showed them proudly to my friends at school.

Now, after so many years, when I look back with nostalgia, I appreciate the happy days the Regiment gave us kids. The whole Regiment was one big family. We could romp and roam around in any nook or corner, only to be pampered, and spoilt. We were taken to the langar (mess) to eat hot 'pakodas' (fritters). The Regiment taught us to be happy, carefree, generous, giving and sharing. Attributes so rare to find and learn in today's world.

Open Letter to My Daughter

Dear daughter,

You were born on a cold winter January morning, at the military hospital Wellington, in the Nilgiris. As I stared at the small tiny infant, my daughter, I thanked God for his miracle. From that moment onwards, your mother nursed you every moment, every day and night. I saw you grow from an infant, to a baby, to a toddler who learnt to take her first steps, to a sweet little girl, and blossom into womanhood.

I was at Matilda hospital Hong Kong, when again on a cold winter November morning, you gave birth to your son. I saw you nurse little Parth day by day. I saw your mother and you selflessly sacrifice all your comforts. These are sacrifices and relentless hard work that only a mother can do. Sitting up night after night when their babies were crying, and looking after every small need.

While you were growing up, I was busy with my work, and did not realize the moment to moment attention, which your mother had to give you. Now that the hectic pace of life has slowed down, I saw you painstakingly look after Parth, cherish him, and love him, with all your heart. When we grow up, we become self-sufficient, and often forget what went into those early years. A mother can never be repaid, and we must love and respect her, and give her a special place in our hearts.

When as a small boy I went to school, I found myself and the other boys, compete at every step. We competed in studies, we competed in sports, competed in each and every thing. As a young man I compared myself with others. I spared no efforts in being first amongst equals. Life became a rat race. As I grew older, I realized that there was nothing noble in being better than the man next to me, there was nothing great in going ahead of the man beside me, that true nobleness true greatness was in competing with yourself, in bettering yourself every day of your life till the very end.

For the better part of my life, I strove to acquire material goods. Expensive cars, branded clothes, and the best gadgets. Showing them off to my friends gave me happiness. As the years went by, I understood that the joy of material possessions was fleeting and faded away fast, leaving you with the desire to acquire more and more. True and lasting happiness came not in getting things for yourself, but in giving. In educating a needy but deserving child, in helping a suffering person, in feeding the poor and hungry. Money spent for humanity is far more gratifying, than splurging on yourself.

You are in the prime of your life. After having spent the better part of my life, and being now in my golden years, I have experienced the twists and turns that life takes us through. There will be successes and failures, people closest to you will drift far away and families which were once very close, may fall apart. The way forward is to be optimistic, follow your conscience, have faith in your own values, keep your head high and live. Leave regrets behind and wipe out bitterness and the thought of being wronged.

God has given us life and a beautiful world. Enjoy every moment of it and leave behind a clean slate. Regrets are a burden, best left behind. Wipe out bitterness and thoughts of being wronged. As you near the latter years, you realize that unhappiness is brought on by bitterness and jealousy. Love reigns supreme, and helps bring peace in the sunset years.

Attachment is the cause of much sorrow. We become very attached and close to our near and dear ones. Our children will grow up, and have their own families, own lives. Of course, they will love you and care for you, but may not come up to your expectations. Don't fret and worry about them and do not get disturbed by their lapses.

You will be left only with your spouse who is the one who cares most for you. Be kind and considerate to each other, look after each other. Bring as much happiness as you can to your soul mate. You will be with one another in health, in illness, in happiness and sorrow. You will always hold each other's hand.

Affectionately,

Your,

Baba.

Dumela

.... the toast was drunk with raised glasses saying 'Pula', and it was invitation for the rain to come.

It was a beautiful autumn day of September in 1980. After having a chicken hamburger and cold coffee in the second floor cafeteria of South Block, I returned to my office room on the ground floor. I was greeted by Sia Ram, my head clerk with a letter, that asked for my willingness to go on a deputation posting to Gaborone, Botswana. My first reaction was where exactly is Gaborone? It reminded me of a similar reaction when my then finance informed me that our wedding would be in Kotagiri, a place I had not heard of. I picked up the telephone and rang up my wife Narayani, who was working as an editor in Prentice Hall, a multinational editorial company in Connaught Place, New Delhi. After a quick check she informed me with glee, Gaborone was in Botswana, Africa and had a strong currency. Of course, I should give my willingness! Being a National Defence Academy fauji (army personnel) I had not given a thought to this angle. Thank God, for my 'civilian' wife!

We were twenty of us, with a Lt Col leading a team of majors and captains from different arms and services. We were on a two year deputation to Botswana to impart training to the Botswana Defence Force (BDF). All expenses, for the entire deputation was to be met by the BDF. We were to fly next month in October, time was short, and there was so much to do. Our five year old daughter Bashuli, studying in lower kinder garden in Army Public School, promptly informed me that there was no need for her to go to school from the next day, as after a month, she would be going to a new school! Narayani would not allow it. The team leader, a die-hard infantry man from Rajputana Rifles and I, reached the Air India office to purchase twenty first class tickets (courtesy BDF). The cute young girl at the counter was wide eyed when she saw the twenty first class vouchers, and immediately whisked both of us away to a posh cabin. On being offered tea or coffee the team leader who was enjoying every bit of it replied "I drink only water, or whisky."

Our Air India flight was on 20th of October at 7AM from Santa Cruz airport Bombay. The ground staff ushered us to the 1st class lounge. While we relaxed munching delicious snacks, and sipping the choicest of beverages, the boarding cards were brought and handed to us. The Boeing 707 First class cabin had a total of twenty seats, and we occupied all twenty. After a flight of eight hours over the Indian Ocean we touched down at Lusaka in Zambia. We spent the night there, and the next evening, we boarded a Dakota aircraft for a two hour flight to Gaborone, the capital of Botswana. As we landed the spectacular view of the setting sun over the acrid desert painting the terrain saffron, was indeed, a gorgeous welcome from Gaborone! The airport, a cluster of hutments in the midst of a near desert, made us wonder whether we were to spend the next two years, in the desert of darkest Africa? On approaching the building, a group of officials approached us saying, "Dumela!". Thereafter, wherever we went people said, "Dumela"; we later learnt that it is a way of greeting in Setswana the language in Botswana. The officials collected our passports to get the immigration formalities completed, and we were escorted to Mercedes limousines, which took us to the five starred Holiday Inn. After spending a month in the hotel, we moved to houses allotted to us.

Botswana is a landlocked country in Southern Africa. It has a landscape defined by the Kalahari Desert and the Okavango Delta, which becomes a lush animal habitat during the seasonal monsoon. It is home to numerous animals including giraffes, cheetahs, hyenas and wild dogs. The climate is semi-arid. Cattle are the traditional source of wealth and status. Botswana is abundant in natural resources such as diamonds, silver, copper, nickel and iron ore. Their currency Pula (meaning rain), in 1980s, was very strong. We were invited to every official function which the President hosted; *the toast was drunk with raised glasses saying Pula, and it was invitation for the rain to come.* The loudest toast to Pula was by the Indian Army Training Team not because of the rain but because Pula was a strong currency!!

Two days after our arrival my wife admitted our five year old daughter to Thornhill School, a high-end school in Gaborone. Within no time my daughter Bashuli was at home amongst the African and European children. It speaks volumes for the hospitality starting at a very young age in the people of Botswana. The Batswana (name for people of Botswana) are very simple at heart and live for the day. Our house was duplex with the bedrooms on the first floor and the kitchen on the ground floor. Early one morning when my wife went downstair to the kitchen to make tea, to her consternation she found the window wide open, food and beer cans thrown all around and a man fast asleep on the floor! She came running up, caught my hand, and took me down. My first impulse was to call the police; but on second thoughts, I gently woke up the man, and in broken Setswana, asked what he was doing here? Without any guilt, he said that last night, feeling very hungry, seeing our window open and not wanting to disturb us, he entered our kitchen through the window. He had helped himself to food and beer from the fridge, and then fell asleep. He thanked my wife and me for our hospitality, said good bye, shook my hand and left. On looking around we found that not a pin had been removed. In the early eighties theft was an unknown word in Botswana. They were simple people who believed in living life, being content and trusting each other. It was a rich country, by virtue of their diamonds, silver, nickel, copper, iron ore and beef exports. Botswana, having earlier been a British colony, was now run mostly by expatriates from the UK, besides India, and Canada. The Batswana earned good money on casual jobs and enjoyed themselves. The shopping complexes were full of plush malls comparable to the best in Europe.

On completion of two years of deputation we were all set to come back. One morning I was called to the headquarters and told that a case would be taken up with the Indian government if I gave my willingness to extend the deputation by another two years. Narayani was thrilled, she had a well paid job, used imported cosmetics, bought beautiful curios, ate Swiss chocolates and cheese, drove a Chevrolet car, travelled on holidays around the world, on kind courtesy the Botswana government; on official passport and first class air tickets.

The extension ended before we realized it and once again much to my amazement, I was offered another extension. I had already been delayed for command by two years. It took all my persuasion to convince my dear wife that it was time to go home and made her laugh by saying that by staying any longer she was likely to get curly hair! So ended a dream tenure. On return while walking in Connaught Place my daughter saw an African girl and went running to her shouting "friend, friend!" Our stint of four years in Botswana had garnered a special bond not only with the Batswana, but with all the people of Africa. It also instilled in Narayani and me the love and joy of travel, seeing new places. and meeting people of different countries. Thank you, the Indian Army and Botswana Defence Force, for this wonderful experience!

Whats App – Boon or Liability

*Our "best" friend has held us fully
captive.*

Today, what is the senior citizens best friend? More than the TV, his companions, indeed even more than his spouse! Technology has brought a great boon to the lives of the silver generation. In the yesteryears, books, music, writing, travelling, formed part of the daily life of the retired gentry. Such activities enriched their lives and gracefully heralded the aged to the mellow years. It added to their wisdom, grace and dignity. Grandchildren received loving letters from their grandparents full of life's experiences and lessons. Beautifully written, each word aptly placed. The letters were cherished for years to come, in fond remembrance of the bygone days. Elders sat together and discussed history, books, authors, music, artists. Birthdays and anniversaries were remembered, greeting cards carefully chosen, and meaningful words conveyed.

Gone are those days. Always beside us is our "best" friend the mobile, housing the magic appliance the mighty WhatsApp. The WhatsApp has the first priority on our time, over and above everything else. On waking up in the morning, freshening up, the newspaper, the morning cuppa are all secondary. The mobile kept safely besides us on the bedside table is grabbed and the WhatsApp opened. The messages are read in great haste and eagerness, and must be attended to immediately. Throughout the day the mobile is clutched tightly in our hands. Messages are received every minute. After all there are so many groups. The college group, the school group, the National Defence Academy course group, the squadron group, the Corp group. Groups, and groups, and more groups. All must be attended to immediately. Doesn't matter if they all contain the same jokes, the same forwards, the same political tit bits. Mundane comments, comments on comments. The forwards are uncanny in their similarity. They all repeat health bulletins or words of great wisdom that have been doing the rounds for the past many years. Replies are shot off profusely thanking those "dears" forwarding the mundane forwards. This is followed by another round of profuse thanks for the thanks. Not one original, not one creative, all just meaningless. ***Our "best" friend has held us fully captive.***

Undoubtedly the WhatsApp is a great boon if used judiciously. On the other hand, the WhatsApp, if allowed can dominate our lives and prove to be a nuisance. The choice of use is left to us.

Mataji

*Mataji was loved by all, and that is
how, as her son, I remember her.*

Every day, at eight in the morning, you would find her
sitting on a canvas folding chair, in a shaded corner of a
plot of land. A lady who was just forty-seven years old; she
was petite, dainty, beautiful and dignified with white
streaks in her hair. Her husband had retired from service a
few months ago. Being the eldest in the family, and having
lost his father early, it fell on him to educate his seven
siblings, in addition to and bringing up his four children.
On retirement he found himself without a home.As Uttar
Pradesh government was selling land on concessional rates
to retired army personnel, he bought land in Lucknow to
build himself a home. He was fortunate to find a job in
Bhopal, an overnight journey from Lucknow. The money
would be useful in building the house. His wife Annapurna,
whom he had married when she was just fifteen years old,
blossomed into an intelligent, resourceful woman, and true
to her name, managed her meager resources to run a happy
home. Now once again, it became her unwavering
commitment to stand steadfast with her husband, and build
their home in his absence. During her wedding ceremony,
she had looked at the North Star, and taken a vow to stand
steadfast with her husband, as the North Star stood in the

sky. Her elder daughter was married and the younger daughter in college. Both her sons were working, and so, here she was every morning supervising building of her house.

I was her younger son and an officer in the Army. I spent my entire leave at her side. Every morning we walked 2km from our rented house to the building site, armed with our lunch and water. She spent the whole day there overseeing the laying of every single brick. At five in the evening, she counted the wages, one note at a time, and paid the workers. Soon all the work men and people in that area came to know her, and being endeared with her demeanor and nature, named her Mataji. It was said, that if Mataji stood for election, she would certainly become the Member of the Legislative Assembly of Daliganj constituency. After paying the daily wages, Ma and I walked back the 2 km to our rented house. After a bath, she cooked our dinner. It would be a simple dinner, sometimes just rice and dal, but whatever she made for me would be with love and affection, and I loved her cooking! After dinner on some evenings, she would sit with her harmonium and sing 'Rabindranath Sangeet' in her melodious voice. Next morning, it was back again to brick and mortar.

My father who loved his wife dearly, named their house Annapurna in her honour. She loved their home and lived very happily with Baba for twenty years. Their love was apparent in simple ways like sharing a 'Limca' every afternoon at 4 PM. Then Baba suddenly took ill, and died within three months. Ma a very strong lady grieved in solitude, without displaying her grief to the world. She stayed on alone in her house with her faithful maid and the maid's daughter for the next ten years. My wife, daughter and I spent all my leave with her. Then ill health took its toll, and her last few years were spent with her elder son and daughter in Mumbai, till God took her to be with her beloved husband. Ever since Baba died, Ma had entrusted me to look after all her monetary and house affairs. She was very meticulous and the Will she left behind with me was very clear as to what she wanted. Her children respected her every wish, and as the executer of the Will, I was able to execute the Will within three months. Due to certain circumstances, I had to sell the house that she and I loved. The buyer was a God-fearing and good person. That went a long way in reducing my pain of parting with the house. We all come to this world, and we will all go away one day. We leave behind our relationships with people. Mataji was loved by all, and that is how, as her son, I remember her.

Stars

I owe my career, courses, promotions, and awards to my fascination with stars.

Ever since I was born, stars in some form or the other, have played an important role in my life. As a baby I went to sleep listening to stories of stars in the sky. As a toddler, I loved to gaze at the stars, while playing outdoors under the clear summer sky. In primary school, I looked forward to my teachers marking my work with a star. I joined the Scouts to learn about constellations. My most memorable gift as a teenager was a telescope, to which I remained glued for hours, at the cost of my studies. In senior the Cambridge class I was thrilled to find " The First Men in the Moon" by HG Wells as a prescribed text.

On being commissioned into the Armoured Corps, we spent many a night, covering long distances in tanks across stretches of desert terrain, with few or no landmarks. Those were the days before the advent of the GPS, when the compass and stars were our guides. I loved such exercises as it gave me a chance to be with my best friends, the stars. As I progressed in service, I was fascinated to see high ranking officers with stars on their cars. Stars shining against the striking backgrounds of either red, maroon, sky blue or navy blue, depending on the service. Some have one star, some two, a very few three and the three service chiefs, the God's own, the coveted four stars. A Squadron Commander of my regiment told me that if I was to ever get stars, I had to be Defence Services Staff College (DSSC) qualified. That meant clearing the dreaded DSSC examination. I was so fascinated with stars that no other motivation was required. *I owe my career, courses, promotions, and awards to my fascination with stars.* After retirement I was devastated that there would be no more stars in my life.

But I soon found to my immense joy that all was not lost. On the golf course golf caps had stars on them! Retired officers were invited to formal functions depending on the number of stars, they carried while in service. Bravo, stars still remained a part of my life!

As I sit in my veranda of cottage number 5, Wellington Gymkhana Club sipping my evening cup of tea I see all the " starred" committee members coming to the " At Home" for selecting aspiring new members. First come the one stars, followed after a suitable interval by the two stars, and finally the three stars. After the " At Home" there will be a scramble for the cars to leave in the reverse order, the three stars first.

After retirement the fortunate leave their stars behind and reclaim the wonders of the twinkling stars of their childhood days. The not so lucky ones have the " quick fix" refusing to come off. They have to bear the cross of the stars for the rest of their lives. May God be kind to them.

Ami Buro Hoa Galam

Burn your candle at both ends it may
not last the night; but O my friends. it
does give a lovely light.

My paternal grandmother, 'thakurma' as we called her, stayed with us. As a young boy, I associated my thakurma with the words, "baba re, ami to buro hoa gelam" (my dear, I have become old). In those times, grandparents stayed with their children and they formed a part of the family. As children, we associated anyone above sixty-five years of age as old. They were supposed to pray, meditate, read books on religion, and on our demand, tell us stories, at best they went on a constitutional walk. We did not need to read the great epics, the Ramayana or Mahabharata, as the stories we heard from our grandparents taught us everything. This was my impression of the aged as I grew up.

My wife Narayani, stayed with her maternal grandparents as a young girl, since her father served in the foreign service, he had to spent many years abroad on diplomatic missions. Her grandfather, 'dadu' as she called him, had suffered two heart attacks. His grand daughter, my wife, whom he called lovingly "my darling", was the apple of his eye. Dadu attended every sports day and swimming meet to see his darling take part, and cheered as if his darling was an Olympic champion. Be it hot or humid in the Kolkata weather, Dadu just had to be there. When she stood on the victory stand, he went ecstatic with joy! He knew all her friends, and was very popular with all of them. They use to vie with each other to buy him goodies at the school fete, from their pocket money. He was their best friend, and enjoyed every moment of it! Dadu, defied age, defied his heart condition, and of course, after taking precautions, loved and lived life to the full. The children adored him, and his friends loved his company. 'Didima' as she called her grandmother, was cajoled once in a while, to permit him to have a drink. He enjoyed living, and the joy of life. That is how Dadu is remembered today. These are the two very different perspectives I had of the aged.

Life went by, high school, college, marriage, family. On retirement I settled in a colony where a large number of retired people live. Once again, I came in close proximity with the aged. I love to observe life and could not but notice how each person's attitude varied on ageing. My curiosity prompted me to do a survey. During evening walks within the colony like-minded people sit in groups on the parapet walls doing 'gup shup' or chatting. On asking the varied age groups as to what old people should do, I received a whole range of answers! Many said old people should not drive, should not travel, restrictions formed a part of most answers. Some replies bordered on the very disquieting, "the old should die!" The replies reflected society's indictment of the elderly. The cultural message that was widespread was be afraid, very afraid of getting old.

Amongst my friends a few are optimistic and others pessimistic. I find that my pessimistic friends fall ill often. Negativity even affects your handwriting and memory, increases chances of getting dementia and many of them even die at a younger age. The conversation amongst the pessimistic is invariably about illnesses, symptoms, medicines. Depressing, indeed very depressing.

Then there are my optimistic friends who lead an active life, golfing, swimming, and exercising in the gym. A few even participate in marathon races at the age of seventy! Travelling frequently, leading social work activities, heading forums and clubs, reading, writing, and socializing. They seem to be winking at life and living with the motto, "come catch me if you can!" Statistics will show that optimism leads to a better way of living life, better health, and longevity. Childhood, youth, middle age, and old age form different segments of our lives, and each age is meant to be lived and enjoyed. Old age has its own charms; freedom from being tied down to time, no deadlines to be met, all responsibilities completed. Hobbies can be pursued, hidden talents found and unleashed. Age is not measured in years is a cliché often heard, but not entirely true as the number of years do take a toll on the body. As medical science has advanced beyond recognition old age problems can be well looked after. Longevity has increased and even a hundred can be imagined. In Sena Vihar, our colony, lives Col Subramanian, 102 not out, mentally and physically robust! Not far behind is Mrs Nath, who has completed a century! The very best must be made of these sunset years. We have two perspectives to choose from, "ami buro hoa galam" or to live up life like Dadu did, and savour a single malt once in a while. The choice is ours to be afraid of the advancing years, or to enjoy life till we fade away with a smile on our face, and a prayer on our lips. I have taken my choice. ***Burn your candle at both ends it may not last the night; but O my friends. it does give a lovely light.***

Rejected

There is a life beyond failure, a life beyond retirement.

One afternoon, in early March 1990, I was busy working in the Military Secretary's branch office in South Block, New Delhi. All of a sudden, I found an exodus towards Sena Bhavan, the Army's Headquarters, two hundred yards away. The herd instinct is ingrained in each one of us, and I too, rushed towards Sena Bhavan. On reaching, I found a ghastly sight. On the ground floor lobby lay the mangled body of a Maj Gen, who had jumped from the seventh floor, and committed suicide. Results of the number one selection board for promotion to the rank of Lt Gen had been announced earlier that morning. He was an above average officer from the very beginning and had sailed through, till now. This morning the word *rejected* stared him in the face for the very first time.

Every officer lives with the fear of when he will face this dreaded word. The word itself is distasteful. In one stroke it changes the course of a service officer's life. From that moment onwards, from being a good officer, he will be categorized as superseded. Suddenly from the most coveted appointments, his postings will be to unwanted positions, which are looked down upon. He will be considered inferior to anyone who is a rank higher than him. His wife and children will live in lower grade houses, than those who are his contemporaries. The rank differential will follow him even in retirement. Like a shadow his rank will follow him till he takes his last breath in an army hospital where he will be given a bed based on his rank. The mortuary will be the first leveler, where all dead bodies are together, with no distinction. When all counting is done, and there remains only a handful of ashes; God will do the final assessment of Approved or Rejected, which will determine our places in heaven or hell.

A few, unable to withstand the transition from the approved to the rejected status, take the untoward step of committing suicide. Large numbers become disgruntled and go into depression, with plummeting self-esteem. This is not being said cynically, and is certainly not a critical appraisal of the armed forces. I love the institution of the Indian Army; having spent forty years in it, from the age of sixteen, when I joined the National Defence Academy. If I was to choose a career again, it would be the army.

Due to the steep pyramidal structure, the best of the best, the cream of the cream, will inevitably be faced with the word rejected. During the opening talk given to my Defence Services Staff College batch, by the then Commandant, Maj Gen AM Sethna, in 1976, he said "I address the cream of the cream, but within this cream much against my wishes, grades will have to be given. Let this not deter you in your learning process or self-confidence." The passage of time notwithstanding, his words ring clearly in my ears. From that very moment, I decided, never to let my own self opinion, esteem, confidence, and worth, be in the hands of another person.

From childhood and throughout our lives, we train ourselves for success. We are not programmed or trained for failure. We do not understand the tremendous power failure unleashes in us. There is no such thing as failure. *There is a life beyond failure, a life beyond retirement.* There are better avenues, if one door closes, another one will surely open, we have only to knock. Our self-esteem, self-respect and self- confidence are our own, no selection board, no society can determine them. In each one of us we have hidden core talents. It is up to us to have the courage to find them and develop them. In service we march along one road for years. In failure, so many avenues open up. Throughout your life you may have had a flair for music, for writing, for speaking, photography, for being a collector of antiques, for entrepreneurship in business, and social work. Any of these paths will bring you more success and satisfaction than you ever found in your chosen career, however far you reached.

Colonel Satya Pal Wahi held the rank of colonel in the army in the Corps of Electrical and Mechanical engineers. On stepping out he was a former chairman of Oil and Natural Gas Commission and the Cement Corporation of India. Chetan Bhagat a banker, left banking and took to writing in which field his books have become best sellers. AJ Cronin was a physician by profession and later became an author of repute.

Closer home, we have Captain Jayanto Kumar Sengupta from the 16 Light Cavalry, who lost sight in both eyes in 1965 Indo Pak war and was boarded out from the army in 1967. It brought to an abrupt end, the brilliant career of a triple gold medalist from the Rashtriya Indian Military

College, National Defence Academy and Indian Military Academy. In 1990, Jojo as Capt Sengupta was popularly called founded the North Bengal Council for the Disabled (NBCD). In 1998, he founded Prerana which flourished into a major pan India Disabled Education organization. Jojo was born with the ability to fight back. He did not know what Rejection was!

Deepa Malik was another of the same breed. I first met Deepa when she came as a very young bride to Bikaner where her husband Vikram was posted in my Brigade Headquarters. She was refreshingly full of life with a zest for joy. Early in life she was inflicted with a serious spine problem which forced her to a wheel chair. She is the first Indian woman to have won a silver medal in the 2016 Summer Paralympics in shot put.

Many of my colleagues having been shown "rejected" cards stepped out into corporates and other fields and are flourishing, happy, and leading contented lives. Many have become depressed, frustrated, and disgruntled. On hearing that I had been rejected, my wife laughed and made me realize day after day, that nobody could approve or reject me, except myself. Only I, and I alone, could determine my own worth. I found the courage, because of her, to hone my talents and today, I am writing, publishing, and giving talks. There is no such thing as being approved or rejected. Give whatever you have within you to the world and "Die Empty", as in the book by Tood Henry. Bring happiness to others and to yourself, and lead a life which makes you happy and contented. Enjoy to the hilt the musical dance of life, which is a gift God has given you.

The Trophy

The trophy was a symbol of a life time achievement. An achievement of having loved, and being loved.

It was still dark outside whilst I sipped my morning tea. The Sena Vihar Golf Tournament tee off was at 7 am. Being a retired officer's colony, majority of the golfers were senior citizens. I was cheerfully waved off by my wife with the words that playing and enjoying the game were more important than winning.

The golf course was buzzing with activity. Golfers were socializing, taking practice swings and exercising to warm up. Caddies were cleaning golf balls, polishing the clubs, and securing the sets on trolleys. After the customary briefing by the organizers, the players teed off. Being a Stapleford tournament, it was a level playing field. Each player played to his handicap. My fourball consisted of thoroughbred golfers, following golf etiquette, knowing rules, courteous, and pleasant. There cannot be a bigger leveler than a game of golf; one day you play like a champ, and the next can be a disaster. Humbleness is a trait worth acquiring and, keeping your head down is the very first lesson taught in golf. Integrity is always on test as the temptation to move the ball just a wee bit, for a better shot is forever looming. It was my lucky day, when I played like a champ, and enjoyed every one of the eighteen holes!

The highlight of a golf tournament is the prize distribution ceremony over drinks and dinner with spouses in attendance. Golfers are a breed apart, having a group of golfers together is in itself a real treat to savor! Put them together, and be assured of an endless banter of golf stories, jokes, anecdotes, and incidents. The prize distribution took place amidst much cheering, back slapping, and drinking of toasts. The winners were made much of, and had not one but many for the road.

Next morning, sitting on my favorite chair, sipping our ritual cup of tea, my eyes fell on the trophy I had won the previous night! It adorned the place of pride in our home, where the most meaningful things of our family were kept. My wife who over so many years had seen me off with a smile saying winning did not matter, playing did, knew only too well what winning just once meant to me. It was moment of realization that the trophy was more than the golf trophy. ***The trophy was a symbol of a life time achievement. An achievement of having loved, and being loved.***

Talk Your Way to the Top

Knowing what to say, how to say it and what not to say will draw people towards us.

Do you remember how it feels to try to listen as someone drones on and on? It may be just that the person you are conversing with is boring you because he is talking all about himself, about stories you don't care to listen to, and about people you have never met! What if that person who is boring you to tears, is YOU? Let's be honest about ourselves, and see the kind of conversation we make.

Do you find yourself constantly offering your opinion when it is not asked for? When you continue to oppose the views of your listener, you run the risk of his not enjoying the conversation. By constantly opposing, you make the person feel wrong, stupid, or uninformed. When someone interrupts you, you know that he is not interested in what you have to say. He believes what he is saying is more important than what you have to say. Interrupting is a disastrous trait. Not interrupting others, could be the single most important part of good-communication.

You say "I got an article published". Your friend responds "I too got five articles published". If you find yourself always looking to compare, it will take away the essence of conversation. If you are a chronic complainer, you will create negative feelings in others, and will push people away from you. Nobody wants to be constantly burdened with your problems. Complaining is best avoided. Sometimes we make it a habit of judging others. Judging others is a giveaway, that you have issues of incompetence and insecurity.

Throughout our lives we communicate with parents, siblings, friends and at work. *Knowing what to say, how to say it and what not to say will draw people towards us.* Keeping away from the 'do not' of conversation will bring happiness, joy and success in our lives. So, let's talk our way to the top.

Joy of Life

Thanking God for all He has given, and accepting all that He has not.

Standard one, six years old. Young boys eagerly waiting for the bell to ring when we would go charging out for the fifteen minutes break. School meant fun, making friends,learning new things, going out for nature study trips, having school picnics on Saturdays. Ma giving us yummy food and Baba (father) bringing back presents when he returned from long trip. On the way back home from school,first a quick visit to the plaza and convince the maid to buy us a pizza. Sundays meant excitement with cricket matches, and eating out with parents. Foreign countries to be visited during summer holidays. The joy of childhood! The age when you are expected to make mistakes. An age when you are encouraged to try out new things and learn from your mistakes. An age when your curiosity has no bounds and all your questions are answered. So many things being seen for the first time. You are encouraged by your parents and teachers to ask the question "why". God's beauty unfolding before your eyes. All your needs being met. Not a care in the world. You have been brought into a wonderful world. You are experiencing the joy of living.

A high school social. You are a teenager eagerly awaiting adulthood. Your first dance. The thrill of for the first time holding a girl in your arms. A new experience. The exuberance of life. The blue sky, the bright sunshine. The first love letter. The world appears as a wonderful dream. A dream where you are living in a Disney land of your own.

College life, new exposure of staying in a hostel, new friends, first taste of freedom, bubbling with ambition, deciding on which career you want. First taste of competition, thriving to be first among equals, disappointments, exhilarations. Growing into manhood or blossoming into becoming a woman. Your first job. Your first girlfriend. Your first date. Money in your hands. Malls, movie halls, restaurants, travels. The world at your feet. You feel the joy of life.

A new chapter of life with marriage and the bliss of married life. The joy and happiness on becoming a father. Seeing your child grow up. The excitement of the first steps. First day in school. The pride in seeing your child receive his first prize, his first trophy. Sports Day in school and your child participating. Oh, the joy of seeing your baby grow from an infant to a toddler, a boy, a teenager and a handsome, capable young man. The thrill of meeting the challenges and getting ahead in the race of life. The urge to earn more and more to rise further and higher. The exhilaration at each success. The satisfaction of being able to give your family the best. The need to be better than the man next to you.

Stepping into retirement. Spending the time, you always wanted to with your spouse. The pleasure of aging together.

Pursuing all the hobbies you wanted to. Golfing with your friends, travelling, seeing your own country, the world, meeting people of different countries. All the time for reading, writing, hearing music, seeing theatre. Being in the company of people you like and who give you happiness. Having silver hair, the dignified look which comes with age, the wisdom gained from experience. Leaving behind all your baggage of having been wronged, bitterness, vengeance. Being at peace with yourself. ***Thanking God for all He has given and accepting all that He has not.***

IT

My mother was looking for a suitable place for IT. From my childhood as far as I can remember IT was always called IT.

My father was in a transferable service and we moved to a new place every two to three years. We had recently moved from Jabalpur to Pune. I was ten years old. The government allotted us accommodation, sometimes very good and at times, modest. Whatever the accommodation, my mother a homemaker by instinct, made it comfortable for each one of us. In today's world ours was a big family, my parents, four siblings, which was common in those days, my grandmother (thakurma), Rashbehari (our helper), and of course a place for IT was always given importance. My mother a perfectionist by temperament finally found a suitable place for IT. Being the oldest in our home IT was given due respect and well looked after. My mother had taught her children not to disturb IT. Next to IT in age was Rashbebari Mohoto. A resident of Muzafarpur in Bihar, he had been my grandfather's helper from the time he was a young boy. When my father got married, Rashbehari was sent with him to help out in household matters. I had seen him from the time I was born and called him "Bhai", and in turn, he called me "Dada Babu." I had grown up being carried on his shoulders and taken for walks. He was very fond of me, and irrespective of how busy he was, he would always find time to attentively listen to me, and engage in conversation. On looking back now I can say with conviction that Bhai had mastered the art of conversation, without ever having heard the word soft skills, let alone attended workshops and webinars. One day I asked Bhai to tell me about the earlier times of IT. He sat me down comfortably and ran to the kitchen to make me some pakoras, which he knew I simply loved. That was how my Bhai was and everyone loved him for that. He then sat down on the floor to tell me the story about IT.

My paternal grandfather (thakurdada), was a doctor. Quiet and reticent by nature, peace loving by temperament. He was a respected doctor and rose to the position of Civil Surgeon of Cooch Bihar in West Bengal. Although his position authorized him to a Chevrolet limousine he went walking to work and back every day. In those days walking was the norm. One day when he returned from work, he brought IT back with him. IT was slim and good looking. IT was to stay with Thakurdada in his room, and Rashbehari was put in charge of taking care of IT. So, from that day onwards IT and Thakurda stayed together. IT accompanied Thakurdada where ever he went. During his morning and evening walks, Thakurdada invariably had IT as his companion. As Thakurdada grew older he got more and more attached to IT and as time went by old age crept in. Gradually Thakurdada grew weak and was unable to walk. When his end came, he called my father and mother and said he was leaving IT in their care. He was very fond of my mother, having chosen her for his eldest son, and brought her as young bride of fifteen to his home as his Bouma (daughter in law). He knew his Bouma would look after IT very well. That is how IT came to our home. I was not born at that time.

When my father (Baba) remained in service IT was quite lonely. A few years after Baba retired, he started spending more and more time with IT. We had settled in Lucknow after Baba's retirement. Every evening Baba and IT would go for a constitutional walk to Ramakrishna Math, say prayers and return. In June 1986 Baba was diagnosed with a terminal illness. He took his illness bravely and left us in November, 1986. One day, on his hospital bed, he told my wife and me that IT would be left with us.

When I met with an accident while playing golf, a long and tedious recovery period ensued. During those long days IT was always at my side helping me to get around. During those difficult times, I came to understand how supportive IT can be.

In their sunset years my Thakurdada and Baba had to have the support of IT. I needed IT during my recovery. In a way IT became our companion, our friend. In my family IT will go down from generation to generation. Finally, 'IT' is my Thakurdada's walking stick, and so, IT and will always remain IT, and that is IT!

Assessment

*Assess yourself, assess situations, act,
live, and enjoy the way you want to,
and think right.*

A classroom in a kinder garden school, Miss Neha the young class teacher gives back each toddler their note book, with a kind word. The innocent angels eagerly open their copies, and look for the stars they have got. When the mothers come to take the kids home, the little ones who are clasping their note books, cling to their mothers and say, "mama, mama, see I have got a star". The babies have got their first assessment.

From now on life will be full of assessments. In school, play, work, indeed in every field of life. The image of ourselves will be based on the assessments we get. Our self-esteem, confidence indeed our happiness will all be based on assessments. Assessment of us made by others, if others are happy with us, we will be happy.

Then come situations in life, where you have to make an assessment and take a decision. Your decision can have a deep impact on your life. In 1998 I was posted as the Deputy General Officer of the Maharashtra and Gujarat Area (M & G) Mumbai. The Adarsh scam of Colaba took place at that time. There was a scramble for allotment of flats in this prime area of Mumbai selling at a throw away price. The top brass of the army and influential government officials made a bee line for allotment of flats. M&G Area was the controlling authority and I was the number two man in the organization. I alone felt it was unethical for the M&G Area to get involved in building a housing complex on disputed land and allot flats to the who's who of the services and bureaucratic civil administration.

After assessing the situation I took the decision that the honorable thing to do was ask for a posting out. There was just over a year for me to retire and a move at this point of time would severely affect my domestic life. Besides the huge financial loss of not taking a flat in Colaba the prime location of Mumbai, and carry the regret for the rest of my life, that I was a loser who could not grab opportunities. There was much to lose and everyone felt I was making a grave mistake. Three years later when the flats were almost ready for allotment the Adarsh scam was unearthed and made headlines in the newspapers. Eleven officers of the Headquarters including my relief were jailed and a CBI case initiated.

To stand tall and upright you have to have the ability to assess situations and take decisions. On many occasions you will have to stand all by yourself. Rabindra Nath Tagore's famous song " akla cholo re" brings this out loud and clear. If others do not follow your call, then go ahead all by yourself. You have only one life, and are responsible for your own actions. All the assessments about you, made by others throughout your life, do not have any meaning. What counts is your assessment of yourself. *Assess yourself, assess situations, act, live, and enjoy the way you want to, and think right.*

The one thing sought after most in the world is happiness. When my grandson was small I used to see the small every day things which gave him happiness. As we go through the stages of life our happiness more and more depends on what we consider as success. Is it not indeed weird that the applause and compliments of others forms the basis of our happiness?

In the sunset years of my life, the worldly possessions, bank balance, glory of past positions held, seem a distant past. They don't hold the same joy and happiness. Opinions, compliments, and assessment by others have lost their meaning. Complexion of the word success has taken a different shade. Relations with my spouse, my near and dear ones, company of friends, the chatter of children, the twitter of birds at dawn, add to my happiness. Life has taken a complete turn, from the stars in copy books and seeing the stars in the sky. Possession of worldly goods is no longer important. The peace and quiet of sitting with my family now form my happiness. The word Assessment once so important to me now does not exist in my vocabulary. It has been replaced by Relationships.

Clubs

The finer points of club life, like social etiquette, grace, and culture are fast becoming a thing of the past.

The word club has many meanings but the association that comes to one's mind is a place where people meet. It conjures up pictures of gracious buildings, set up in velvet green lawns, where the soft thud of tennis balls intermingles with the clink of glasses and polite conversation.

Clubs and the idea of clubbing in India is of British origin, probably brought about by their nostalgic need to create an atmosphere of 'home' in a foreign land. It is a meeting place for like-minded people who have leisure and money to indulge their hobbies, be it games, cards, events or local gossip. Clubs in the olden days was a way of life. The membership was restricted and the privileged few got together in the evenings to enjoy themselves in posh surroundings, while liveried waiters catered to their every need. There was a mode of dress and a code of behaviour with strict "dos and don'ts" which added a somewhat gracious, if formal touch. You could go there to eat French fries with tomato sauce, play tombola and borrow books from a library full of books. There are happy hours at the bar, May Queen Balls, and Diwali Melas. A gymkhana club has sports activities.

Clubs are a status symbol. People display their Delhi Gymkhana Club car sticker with pride. It took me twenty-five years to become a member of Delhi Gymkhana Club. It is a place for anybody who is a somebody in Delhi. Being a veteran club hopper having permanent membership of a dozen prestigious clubs, I can say with conviction that the Wellington Gymkhana Club with its scenic beauty and good management is an unbeatable haven for spending a serene holiday. It has an 18-hole golf course and 69 acres of pure bliss in an esoteric fusion of nature and history. The Wellington Gymkhana Club has affiliations with numerous prestigious clubs of this genre, in India and abroad. The main attractions of the club are its sylvan surroundings, sprawling golf course and an inescapable spell of historic charm it casts on the visitors

Another city which was famous for many clubs in the earlier years was Lucknow. The Lucknow Club was established and flourished off the Ashok Marg near the renowned Hazratganj area. This club was mainly for the Anglo- Indian community which found its own place, mid-way between the east and the west. For those who like a bit of local colour, it is said that there were more 'khansamas' (master cooks) than members, who spoke in broken English in imitation of their British masters.

This brings us to the Mohammad Bagh Club in the serene and quiet cantonment area. It was and remains a club for the cantonment, though it does have many civilian members, who play an active part in club life. Its red and cream building with the tennis courts on one side, and the swimming pool on the other is a popular meeting place.

Kolkata has a large number of clubs, with well known ones like the Bengal Club which is still frequented by retired ICS officers and brown sahibs of the British era. Mumbai's Royal Bombay Yacht Club and United Services Club are status symbols. Then there are the Bombay Gymkhana, Willingdon Sports Club, Cricket Club of India and several others.

With the five star hotels and resorts coming up the younger generation are drawn more towards them and club life is losing its charm. ***The finer points of club life, like social etiquette, grace, and culture are fast becoming a thing of the past.***

Inheritance

*Is there any way or an answer to stop
this destruction of the basic fabric of
relationships?*

Asha Guha lived with her son just a few houses away
from ours in a prime locality in Lucknow. The cruel hand
of destiny had snatched her husband away in the prime of
life, leaving her and their ten years old son Dhruv behind.
She was a strong, capable and practical lady, who knew
she would have to bring up her young son, and face the
rest of life all by herself. Her husband Deb had bought a
plot of land and Asha mashima (aunty) took it upon
herself to build a house with the money he had left behind.
Her sweat and blood went into building the house, brick
by brick. It would be a monument in memory of her
husband and a token of love for her only son Dhruv, the
apple of her eye. The years went by and mashima spent
her life looking after every need of Dhruv, meeting all his
wants, needs, whims, fancies, and never thinking about all
the sacrifices she was making. Her world started and
ended with Dhruv, he was all she had, and her life
revolved around him.

Time and tide wait for no man. Dhruv grew up and got
married to a girl of his choice. Mashima did not approve of
his choice but would not do anything which made Dhruv

unhappy. After a few months he moved out to stay in a rented flat much to her dismay. After all the house was built for him. Soon thereafter he began demanding that the house be gifted to him. Her refusal strained their relationship and it did not take long for Dhruv to cut off all relations with his mother. Asha mashima was devastated. Unable to live with this break in relationship with Dhruv her existence seemed futile.

She relented and gifted her house, the only worldly possession she had, to her son. Dhruv sold the house to a developer for a big amount as it was in the prime area of Lucknow, and lived the rest of his life as a wealthy man. Mashima was sent to an old age home to spend the rest of her life. Her monument in memory of her beloved husband, her token of love for her only son was shattered. Asha mashima died a desolate, betrayed woman. The child who had learnt to take his first steps holding her finger, for whom she had sacrificed her life had betrayed her. Her life had been in vain. The inheritance she had thought of leaving behind was snatched away from her by the apple of her eye.

Parents love their children and leave behind their life long treasures to them. Inheritance is a monument of love, and in the earlier times, it was treasured. One generation after another lived in the family house. The inherited home was the heritage and pride of the family lineage. It was associated with our forefathers and their blessings. Mothers gave their most treasured and loved jewelry to their daughters and daughters in law. It was the pride of the family, invaluable and irreplaceable, passed on from one generation to another. These family relics are now treated as outdated. Modern day wives are seen going to upmarket stores to exchange them for new fashionable ones. Inherited jewelry is melted at a loss and new ones ordered. What has come down through ages vanishes without a thought.

Inheritance today is looked upon as a right. It is no more a monument of love left by parents who sacrificed a lifetime for their children. Parents are left to fend for themselves so that the children's dreams can be fulfilled. They are expected to hand over their property and savings to their children during their lifetime. Newspapers are full of sad incidents where inheritance has been the root cause of unhappiness and ruined many a family. Son fights with father, brother fights with brother, property is fought over and families are broken up. Court cases are filed, go on for years, and money flows like water. Inherited jewelry is no longer looked upon as family treasure, instead, it is sold to acquire modern jewelry.

Inheritance has lost its meaning and significance, and looked upon as a source of wealth, which is yours by virtue of your birth, and therefore your right to demand. As wealth to be acquired without earning it, wills are questioned and contested. Inheritance has today become an evil, a curse. Blessed are the families who do not face this problem. Unfortunate are the many families who are afflicted with this malaise. How can this evil be banished so that families can once again live with love without fighting for material wealth? It has destroyed the relationships between brother and brother, sister with sister, broken the hearts of parents, and fragmented families. *Is there any way or an answer to stop this destruction of the basic fabric of relationships?* (Names of people and places have been changed).

Out of Uniform

the choice is ours, whether we keep moving ahead, or put a full stop at retirement

On the day I was to retire, my PA brought to me the form required for retired officers' identity card. In the column color of hair he had entered "black and white". One stroke of the pen had changed a colorful cavalry officer, into a black & white retired person. A week after retiring in an attempt to avoid a traffic jam, I thought of going through an army unit. At the gate I showed the sentry my brand-new retired officers identity card with a flourish, only to be told "sir for serving officers only." Going for golf one morning I responded smartly to a salute, only to realize it was meant for the JCO ahead of me. A few months after adjusting to retired life I decided to have a well-earned holiday in the Nilgiris. After a long drive I went to the bar in the evening all suited and booted to have a tall drink, forgetting it was a serving officers bar! I had a hearty laugh at myself, understanding that this was a transition period from in uniform to out of uniform!

After decades of being in uniform, when we step into civilian wear and mode, we veterans transition into a whole new world, a new phase of life and our second innings. During my welcome dinner, I was advised by several of the retired officers that I had worked hard for many years and now I had earned the right to spend my time playing golf during the day and drinking in the evening.

I choose to leave the past behind and start a new life. Now after twenty years of retirement I realize that there is certainly a life beyond retirement. A life which has much to offer. Perhaps a life better than our first innings, where the glories of the past have much less importance. There have to be new goals, new achievements, and a new identity to be built for ourselves. We have lived a full life and not merely existed; therefore, *the choice is ours, whether we keep moving ahead, or put a full stop at retirement.*

Impressions

*From childhood incidents and people
play a part in our lives and shape our
values, principles, personality and
character*

On 13th September, I celebrated my seventy seventh birthday. I looked back on my life and realized how many impressions had been imprinted on my mind by incidents and people, who had shaped my personality and character.

In the past, parents would put their children in boarding schools at an early age, in the belief that boarding school would gear up the child for life. At the age of nine I was in a boarding school. I remember it was a cold, rainy, Saturday afternoon, enlivened by being a half holiday and 'tuck 'day. We waited the whole week for the tuck day. We children were standing in a que waiting for our turn to come to buy tuck. Two rupees was our quota for the week. Our House master was on tuck duty that day. He announced that our school gardener had been diagnosed with a very serious ailment and needed money for treatment. Any of us who wanted could contribute from our tuck money. The thought whether I should contribute and how much from those precious two rupees raced through my mind. Most of the children ahead of me did not contribute. A few gave four annas. My turn had come. I was standing in front of the House master. On impulse I said softly, sir please take my two rupees. He looked at me with surprise showing in his eyes. He asked, son no tuck this week? I turned back slowly and walked past the children relishing their tuck. Next day in the morning assembly my contribution was announced as an example to others. That impulsive contribution created an impression in my mind. It taught me that to spend on others gives more happiness than spending on ourselves. That one impression taught me to sacrifice again and again. My first Timex watch gifted by my father was given away when my elder brother went to engineering college. Paying the school fees for a needy boy, and seeing the boy grow up to be a capable good young man, filled my heart with joy. A small yearly contribution to a cancer society. Such small contributions brought me happiness.

The army was engaged in counter insurgency operations and the fateful nights are indelible for those who took part in this particular operation. Intense firing was going on in a confined space in built up area. Suddenly one of my men right in front of me got shot in the stomach. His buddy ran forward under heavy fire to carry his friend to cover. He was willing to sacrifice his life to save his friend's life. The spirit of sacrifice to help another notched a permanent place in my mind. A helping hand can be given in everyday life even in small things. Helping an elderly person to cross a busy road or buy medicines. Retrieving the ball of a little boy or offering your seat to a lady in a crowded bus. I learnt that a sacrifice however small, makes our life happy and complete.

The Adarsh scam in Colaba Mumbai hit the headlines in 2010. I was posted in Area headquarters, Mumbai, when the seed of the plan germinated in the minds of the hierarchy in 1999. Land in the heart of Colaba military area had been used to build commercial flats. Flats in Adarsh building were going at throw away prices and naturally there was a scramble for flats. A flat would have been mine for the asking. But I knew in my mind that building the Adarsh was just not right. How could I be part of it? Rather than getting into a tussle with the powers that be who were also my friends I asked for a posting out on certain other grounds. I was the only one not party to the scheme, and all those who knew me wondered how I could let this golden opportunity go by. By mid 2010, the flats had been completed and ready for handing over. It so happened that two of the allotees came to my house for lunch. There was much jubilation amongst them. The market value of the flats was in crores. It had to be as after all the flats were in the prime area of Colaba. My friends looked at me with sympathy as if I had made a terrible mistake. Even my wife who respected my decisions more than anyone else in the world started doubting my action. Then soon after, one morning the newspapers were screaming-Adarsh Scam!! The scam had erupted just before the flats were to be handed over. In all the TV channels prime time news was Adarsh, and only Adarsh. Eleven high ranking officers from the Area headquarters were in jail. Twenty one years have lapsed, but the court case is still in progress. This incident made a deep impression on my mind to always trust my own judgement, and follow my conscious irrespective of what the world said.

From childhood incidents and people play a part in our lives and shape our values, principles, personality and character. That is why it is so very important to have good friends and company. In childhood my mother often told me a Bengali saying --- if you stay with sandalwood the sandalwood rubs off on you and if you stay with moss it will rub off on you.

A Reunion to Rememember

By Narayani Chakravarti

A large number of army wives are from an army background. At the time of my engagement, I fell among the minority community. I had just no army connections, absolutely nil. On coming to know that I would be marrying an army officer the first question that I was invariably asked was "ex NDA?" The first time I gave a blank look but was well prepared thereafter. Early in my marriage I learnt that the National Defence Academy is a prestigious institution of the country from where cadets are trained for the armed forces. I soon found out from my fiancée that the ex NDA are a special breed. He could speak for hours about the three years he spent at the Academy.

My first glimpse of National Defence Academy (NDA) came on a moonlit night after we had been married for just a month. We had driven down in our Lambreta scooter from Ahmednagar where my husband Chaks was posted, to Pune for the Part D examination, starting the next day. After dinner on an impulse, Chaks decided that he must show me NDA. His pamphlet was put aside, the exam forgotten, and we were off. Our first halt was at the Sudan Block, a magnificent sight in the moonlight as was the rest of NDA. It was a dream ride and I came back in a thoughtful mood, and decided never to boast about my college. There is just no comparison, although my college is a Maharaja's palace nestled in the beautiful blue mountains of the Nilgiris.

As the years went by, I understood the deep bonding amongst the ex NDA and more so between course mates. Course mates were like blood brothers, who stand united. So, when the news came of the Golden Jubilee Reunion, I could understand Chak's excitement and jubilation. Although three months away he couldn't wait and preparations had to start immediately. His enthusiasm was infectious and we talked endlessly of the Reunion to come. We were to go back to the NDA after decades. Memories of my first visit as a new bride, on a moonlit night, on a Lambreta scooter came flooding back.

The NDA bus took us to the squadron where we would be staying. We entered Juliet squadron to the joyous sound of laughter and much back slapping. The civilian helpers took our luggage to cabin number 21. These were the cabins where our better halves had spent three years during which time they had bonded with their course mates, shared pranks and punishments and become men from boys. The corridors resounded with remembered stories and incidents and we wives shared in their laughter and gaiety.

On walking into the Cadets Mess I met Pratima Gole, Hem Harish, Mona Mishra and many other friends whom I had known earlier. All young mothers then, and all of us grandmothers now. So much had happened over the years. A lot to catch up and talk about. Maybe grandmothers are but girls at heart, and soon we were busy discussing what clothes we had brought and when we would wear them.

On entering the Mess the grandeur of the place was awesome. The doors at the entrance are made of Belgium glass and the interiors are well furnished. The Mess can seat over 1800 cadets. I was thrilled that I would be having meals here, having heard stories of cadets enjoying sumptuous breakfasts and vying with each other about the number of eggs and toasts they could eat.

Lunch at Peacock Bay was one of the highlights of the Reunion. With the scenic view, beer flowing, tasty snacks,sumptuous lunch, a beautiful sunny morning, meeting friends and making new ones. It was a morning to remember. Our husbands were recalling their NDA days and thoroughly enjoying themselves. The memories of that wonderful lunch are often discussed when course mates meet.

Amongst the whirlwind of events that had been planned the most nostalgic was the visit to the Hut of Remembrance. It is a cenotaph that commemorates the sacrifice of former NDA officers who had given their lives in wars and in the performance of their duties. All of us were dressed appropriately for the occasion and a solemn air prevailed. The veterans approached and entered the Hut in slow march and paid their respects. Ladies also entered to remember the brave hearts who had given their today for our tomorrow. The occasion left a deep impression on all of us.

We had joined the ranks of 'Army Wives' from different walks of life. Many came from army backgrounds and were familiar with the environment, customs and the dos and don'ts. For me it was a sea change having had no services connections whatsoever. But it did not take long to become a part of the Army wives band wagon. Our husband's course mates became our friends. As the years went by the bonding between wives cemented. Our children had grown up together, and we had shared our happy and sad moments. Now we were meeting so many years after retirement. It brought back memories of our earlier years, the happy days we had spent together. The two days we spent together during the Reunion were full of joy and laughter and I will cherish these memories for the rest of my life.

Breaking the Age Barrier

The computer has come as a miracle
into our lives, and brought joy.

Mouse, cursor, taskbar, icons, and a barrage of terminologies are swirling in my mind 24x7. Nagging doubts of whether it was worth it, kept creeping in. I was daring into the world of computers in my seventieth year. Till now I was leading a contented retired life; reading, music, golfing, television; and the joy of being amongst a happy family, helped me enjoy my life. My woes began when my daughter, my only child relocated to Hong Kong. My wife and I could not bear to be out of touch with her for even a day. Long distance phone calls were prohibitive and we constantly worried about our daughter and her family. We grew irritable and felt depressed, gone were the happy days and life was just not the same. As a solution my son-in-law presented me with a brand-new laptop. But operating it was a distant dream for me and the thought of even starting it, sent shivers down my spine, lest I forgot the shutting down procedure. I signed up for a three months computer course, rang up and disturbed my friends' children at odd hours, to clarify the simplest of doubts. Then, I went into shock when my laptop warned "this program has performed an illegal operation and will be shut down." I had a choice. To persist or throw in the towel, and lose touch with my daughter and grandson. I simply had to conquer and vanquish my fears.

With each day I felt more confident. Now six years later I have entered a new era. I am computer savvy. We share our grandson's play dates as if we were there. He shows his Didu (grandmother) the bruise when he fell down during the soccer game. We share stories together on face time. He laughs with us and is consoled by his Didu, when in his words, he is 'not happy'. We read his report card with pride, and celebrate after seeing his swimming certificate. We swell with pride on seeing our sportsman son-in-law's trophies won at regular intervals. My wife has long conversations with our daughter on face time; and, all for free! We are once again part of each other's lives and once again, a happy family!

Now I pay all my bills, do all the bank work, purchase cinema, theatre tickets, air and train tickets online. My wife buys her cosmetics from Marks and Spencer and bedsheets from Maspar, online. Even groceries are purchased on the net. All the hassles of daily chores have vanished like magic. ***The computer has come as a miracle into our lives, and brought joy.*** Today we live in an age where the internet has made the world a global village. Access to information and knowledge is instant and social media connects us to literally thousands of people. Distance poses no barrier to be part of the lives of our near and dear ones.

The colony we live in is for retired people. Most of us have one or more children abroad. Many have not ventured into the world of computers and they do not enjoy the fruits of technology. My wife and I try to spread the word of the whiz-bang miracle called the computer. I ask them, "why should the young have all the fun?" Change is essential and we must change with the times! We enjoyed the past era, now let us make most of the new age. Let us be part of today's younger generation. Let us also have fun. Let's break the Age Barrier.

All the World is a Stage

*Do social norms dictate our lives or is
it the inability to say no?*

I am sitting in a comfortable chair in the Sapphire Toy
Shop, in Bangalore. This has nearly become my permanent
address. You see, my wife Narayani is going through a
phase of buying toys for our grandson, Parth. We make
quarterly visits to Hong Kong and, a lot of the time in
between is spent toy shopping. God is merciful, and my
fixed deposits interests also come quarterly.

As I look around a young mother is eagerly looking for
a super hero. Which one should she buy; Hulk, Spider Man,
Iron Man, or Captain America? A few children are running
around in super hero costumes, shouting "I am a super
hero". Should we as parents, allow a money-spinning
industry to mould young lives? Starting young lives with
pretention, dominated by images, and inflated self-esteem?
Strangely enough, there is no crowd around the book
shelves, the written word no longer seems to matter.

Young parents sporting Polo tee shirts, Levi jeans, Rado
watches, Gucci hand bags, and Boss sun glasses wander
around; while whiffs of Davidoff and Dior perfumes fill the
air. It doesn't matter if the EMIs take a life time, and why
bother if there is an economic crisis and shrinking
availability of jobs? The ruling anthem seems to be we

must have them at any cost; after all, we only live once! Living in a make belief world which really doesn't exist, where the image takes center stage.

Panting grandparents seeing children off on school buses, but isn't this the time to be cosily tucked in bed, resting their tired bones? Grandmothers spending months on end in distant foreign countries baby-sitting, so that the mothers can continue to hold high profile jobs. Their aging husbands fending for themselves looking after their homes instead of spending the sunset years in their own nest? Homes and property of parents being cunningly grabbed, and then parents and the aged being used as menial workers, or thrown out of their own homes. Why, has it come to this? Is it to pretend that we must continue to be good parents and grandparents, no matter what the cost? Is it the inability to say "no" and are we are merely playing out roles as dictated by society?

Children treating parents and elders condescendingly. Pranam? Never heard of it! Whoever does pranam in this day and age? Futile engaging in a conversation with the elderly, after all, what do they know? Values and principles that are outdated in today's world. Character? Meaningless! After all, winning is all that matters. Forgetting our own culture, aping the West, pretending and acting that we are modern. Living on a stage!

Fortunately, our rural areas have not been infected by this malaise. Unless it is nipped in the urban metros and cities, dharma will be replaced by adharma. Imbibing our culture in our children is of the utmost importance to keep our country from ruin and destruction.

God creates each one of us as individuals. Looks, capability, talents, nature, and temperament differ. We spend our childhood and working lives competing, pretending, and acting to be high achievers. Our silver years are spent living the way society expects us to. ***Do social norms dictate our lives or is it the inability to say no?*** Do we live by our own choice or by chance? We seem to have forgotten William Shakespeare's words "All the world is a stage, And all the men and women merely players." Should we act out our roles from entry to exit and then merely fade away, or lead a meaningful life on our own terms?

My Friend Harish

A true soldier who believed that work and friendship had their respective places.

The best leave us first. An age old saying, but so very true. Some of the finest of our course mates were not with us during the National Defence Academy, Golden Jubilee celebrations in December 2014. During my tenure as Dy Ms Army Training Command (Artrac) at Shimla, my job involved working closely with the Liaison officer Artrac, an officer of Col rank stationed at Sena Bhavan, New Delhi. Having to work closely together, I was keen to establish a good relationship with him. That is when I first met Col Lakshminarayan Harish. Although course mates we had not met before. It was not long before I became well acquainted with 'Lattoo Harish' as we all fondly call him. A simple and cheerful man, with moral courage, who shouldered both responsibility and the consequences without fail, if things went wrong. ***A true soldier who believed that work and friendship had their respective places.*** My tenure was made memorable due to the two officers I worked closest with— the Army Cdr Lt Gen SK Sharma, from the 2 Lancers, and Lattoo Harish my friend and course mate. Both, human beings par excellence.

My next posting was as Dy General Officer Commanding HQ Maharashtra & Gujarat Area, Mumbai. Harish whose medical category was upgraded was posted as Commander of the Infantry Brigade at Pune. My work involved frequent visits to Pune. Invariably I stayed with Lattoo. His wife Hemlata, in the AMC was posted at Delhi. He kept his ailing mother like a queen in his Brigade Commander's house. Many an evening I sat with Lattoo, sipping a drink and seeing the albums of his Indian Peace Keeping Force days, commanding 9 Bihar. Obviously a very capable and loved Commanding Officer! Humble to a fault he never spoke of himself, always full of praise for his men and officers. Just like Lattoo! He ran a happy brigade, in keeping with his character, work and fun in their own place. By now we were more than brothers, having met each other's family members and spent many special moments together. My daughter Bashuli and Lattoo were very fond of each other.

On retirement I settled in Bangalore and Lattoo was posted at the Selection Centre. Again, many happy times together. He retired from there and settled in Bangalore. Health let him down and his old cardiac and diabetic problems caught up with him. He fought valiantly, always with a smile on his face, as if death was smiling at him and he was smiling back.

He left behind his wife Hemlatha, a courageous, straight forward, no nonsense, lady of substance. A wonderful person to know. Of his two sons, Vikram settled in London and Swastik in Bangalore. We had the wonderful opportunity of meeting Hemlatha at the Golden Jubilee Celebrations in 2014 in the National Defense Academy. Goodbye my friend, goodbye my course mate!

Birthdays

The pleasures of innocence and being
able to see and enjoy the joy of life.

During November 2020 I attended two birthday parties. Both were very special to me. Twenty years ago, when I first settled in Sena Vihar, on an evening walk my eyes met with a dignified elderly lady. As if by instinct we both walked across the road towards each other. I wished her, addressing her as Madam. She wished me addressing me as "Twinkling eyes." From that day onwards, we remain Madam and twinkling eyes to each other. Both being regular walkers we met every evening and exchanged pleasantries. By and by we became good friends. What I found astonishing about Madam is that she had something nice to say about all of us in Sena Vihar. To her every single person in our colony was wonderful, owners, residents, and staff. This trait in Madam keeps her happy and well, she never talks about her past; it is always about the present and the future.

Madam completed one hundred years in November, 2020. The birthday party started sharp at 5pm. There were twelve of us in all, and at seventy six, I was the youngest. She was standing there straight, upright, and the atmosphere all round was cheerful. It was apparent that all of us were very fond of her; we all made much of her and happiness glowed on her face! On popular request she sang a song for us, a song we will cherish forever. Sena Vihar has brought a lot of happiness to me. But undoubtedly the biggest treasure I have found in Sena Vihar is my friendship with Madam. I have learnt from her that happiness, peace of mind, and good health come from within ourselves. Thank you dear Madam, for teaching us all, how to live.

The second birthday was of my grandson Parth who completed ten years of age on 27 November, 2020. A difference of over nine decades between Madam and Parth. Maturity on one side and innocence on the other. Parth's birthday party with the shrieks of joy from the children running all around brought home the exuberance and innocence of youth. The joy within their hearts. The palpable similarity between the two birthdays was the true joy and happiness both enjoyed and spread to all those around them.

Parth with his grandmother Narayani

In the humdrum of everyday life, we often lose sight of the simple pleasures of life; to laugh, love and live! As the years add up the physical vision gets clouded, but the inner vision awakens bringing back pleasures which we had once enjoyed in our childhood. ***The pleasures of innocence and being able to see and enjoy the joy of life.*** The silver years have a lot to offer and it depends on us to make the most of life as the years go on.

Thank you, Madam and Parth for bringing me back once again to the joys that life can offer, and whatever the odds, we can do it!

The War Within

I realize with a smile that everything in the army may change but not the brave, loving, Army wife.

Sitting in my study, viewing the shelves where my wife has proudly displayed my medals, trophies won and mementoes received, my eyes shift to the Vishisht Seva Medal parchment, signed by former President Shri K.R Narayanan on the wall. Memories spanning over three decades in uniform come flooding back. I go back almost half a century and see myself as a sixteen year old boy proudly entering National Defence Academy as a cadet, full of enthusiasm and bursting with spirit to serve the Indian Army, and my country, as a proud officer.

Four decades later, with salt and pepper hair and a slight stoop, I enter Sena Vihar, Bangalore, a retired army officers' colony, an equally proud and satisfied man, secure in the belief that I will always belong to the great institution of the Indian Army, to which I had given the better part of my life.

A week later, I run into a traffic jam for which the Bangalore roads are well known. The only way to escape is to go through an army organization. I proudly pull out my brand new retired army officers' identity card and with a flourish, show it to the sentry at the gate. He curtly informs me that civilians and retired officers are not permitted entry! I put on a brave front and with a casual air explain to my aghast wife that there must be a good reason for it. After a few months, being an avid golfer, I turn my attention to the membership of a nearby army golf course. Like an eager child, I await to be given membership. After seven years of waiting, I reluctantly realize that as a retired officer, I will not be given a membership. Being a diehard soldier who only saw good in the Indian Army, I got over my disappointment and brushed aside the incident as an aberration.

After a year and the initial rigors of settling down to a retired life, my wife and I decided to have a holiday in the club located in the blue mountains of the Nilgiris. We looked forward to it all the more because it was an army run club and we would be amongst our own kith and kin. After a hard day's drive and a hot bath, we went suited and booted, all complete with my regimental tie, to the bar and ordered a drink. You can imagine my consternation when informed by the bar man (an army jawan) that as a retired officer, I could not be served a drink from the army bar. On enquiring from the secretary, the next day, I was told as a retired officer I was placed in the civilian category!

On the table beside me, next to my 11 o'clock cup of tea, which my wife lovingly serves me every day, are newspapers and magazines with bold headlines of the army pensioner threatening self-immolation on Independence Day. The newspapers and TV are running amuck with news that aged veterans asking for One Rank One Pension at Jantar Mantar, being manhandled by the police. The ex-serviceman is being fast disillusioned from the sense of belonging and there is a constant gnawing at his self-respect. Is this the sadness which makes a once proud father not want his son to join the army or his daughter to marry an army officer? Can our top brass amputate this gangrene and give back to the ex-servicemen, the sense of belonging, self-respect and dignity, on which his whole existence depends?

I am brought back from my reverie with a peck on the cheek by my wife who is clearing the tea cup. *I realize with a smile that everything in the army may change but not the brave, loving, Army wife.*

Financial Fraud

*Let us become aware and beat the
scamsters at their own game.*

We are on our way to a party at a friend's house. As we
enter the room we hear about a friend's wife falling prey to
a net banking fraud. This is not the first. There have been
several other friends who have fallen prey to such frauds
and lost large sums of their well earned money.

During our school, college, and working lives,
computers did not play any role. The desk top or laptop did
not form a an essential part of the house. Then came
retirement. PAs, household staff, drivers, which were taken
for granted during service days, disappeared at the stroke of
midnight on retirement day. Children were not with us.
Household needs, banking, postal requirements, ticketing
were all to be done by ourselves. For the first ten to fifteen
years after retirement, my wife and I did not feel the strain
of going out for our household chores. But later, when we
were in our seventies, age started to take its toll.

Then came the pandemic and going out became
impossible. Some other way had to be found and the
answer lay in going online. Online purchases could bring
any and everything to our doorsteps, by just the press of a
button. There was no other alternative but to learn using a
computer. Using a computer was like learning the alphabets

in nursery school. Many seniors learnt and started using the computer for basic necessities. Covid-19 made visiting banks taboo and banking through net banking became a necessity. Consequently, cyber crimes sprang up in a big way. Fraudsters targeted seniors who were late adapters of technology. Not a week passed without news of cybercriminals targeting older folks above the age of sixty. They have their life time savings in banks. With their trusting demeanor they fall easy prey to fraudsters. KYC updating is one of the top scams for targeting seniors.

Other forms of financial cyber frauds include fake insurance schemes. Scammers know that if they say the right words seniors will do anything to make things right. Fraudsters use kind words, attention, and build up a sense of connection, or else they will frighten, warn, and bully you into relenting. They have all the tricks in the bag to win you over. Being scammed robs a senior of his confidence and self esteem. Many cannot just forgive themselves for being so stupid and giving information away. They have to live with this guilt for a long time. Many feel embarrassed to tell their friends and relatives for fear of being taken as naïve and foolish. Being scammed may psychologically effect and damage a senior. To stop reoccurrence children may stop parents from using technology for financial transactions. Seniors lack the will and energy to follow it up with the cyber crime department police. As a result, an alarming number of cases go unreported. Amongst the cases reported a very small percentage are recovered.

Sena Vihar, where I live, has a large number of seniors residing. To safeguard their valuable money, I felt the urgent need to educate, and spread awareness of the dos and don'ts of computer technology, amongst the seniors of my colony. Consequently, talks are being organized regularly in the Speakers Forum of Sena Vihar. Executives from banks are being invited to visit and speak to residents on the latest techniques being used. Phishing is a common and much used form of scamming. This is an e mail scam where you appear to get a message from a legitimate source such as your bank, Apple, Amazon, or any other. This message will encourage you to click a link and log into your account by telling you that your account has been locked or there has been a large transfer of money. Then there is Vishing in which there is phone call where the scammers pretend to be from your bank or government agency. The caller will try and get you to reveal your personal details.

For seniors their health and financial independence play a very important role. With the world being taken over by technology; it will not be possible to function in our day to day lives, without being abreast with technology. The secret of joyfully living in our senior years is to ensure that our money is safe, and not swindled by the scamster rogues. Let us move ahead with the world confidently without living in fear of scamsters. *Let us become aware and beat the scamsters at their own game.*

Experience of a Lifetime

Consciously thinking about the things that bring me joy, allows me to notice the positives, amongst the doom and gloom.

During the third week of February 2020, my wife was eagerly looking forward to the Konark dance festival with a group of her college friends. It was to be a grand reunion, many of them meeting after five decades or more. Young college girls then, grandmothers now! By that time the creepy fangs of Covid-19 virus were slowly but surely looming over our heads and casting dark shadows over us. Much against her wishes she had to pull out, as many others did to keep away from crowded areas like the airport, aircraft, and the dance festival. She consoled herself that very soon we were to go to one of the highlights of our retired life, our yearly visit to the Wellington Gymkhana Club, in the Nilgiris. Much to our disappointment the Club closed down in the middle of March and the visit had to be cancelled. Covid-19 certainly had affected our life.

On the evening of 24th March 2020, the Prime Minister on a national broadcast announced a nation-wide lock down for three weeks to commence from the next morning. We had not experienced a lockdown. What all did it cover?

What would be the impact? During my over seven and a half decade life, I thought I had seen it all. Wars, riots, floods, earthquakes, the 2003 Hong Kong SARS epidemic, demonetization, and other difficult times. I had never imagined the turmoil that the Covid-19 pandemic would create in my life, and indeed in the world. During the lock down I could not step out of my door. My wife and I did not know where our next loaf of bread, vegetables, or medicines would come from. With no domestic help it was strenuous for the two of us, well in our seventies, to do all the household chores, and cooking. It was our optimism, humor and will power, which kept us going. A week into lockdown saw us with almost no provisions. That was when one morning the door-bell rang. Standing outside the door was a young man may be in his early forties. He wished me and asked if he could be of any help and get me anything. To my wife and me he was a messenger from God. From then on wards, he or his wife rang our door bell every few days, and helped us with our provisions. Often tasty home-made dishes were brought to ease out the strain of our cooking. His wife reminded us of our daughter who lives in Hong Kong and who as much as she wants, is not in a position to be with us. In times of need the goodness in the world comes out, as brought out by this young couple. They simply wanted to help an elderly couple living by themselves in these difficult times. In a sense they adopted us.

Days ran into weeks and weeks into months. Almost five months later, life had taken a different pattern. A new phrase had been coined, the new normal. During this period, I have seen human behavior from close quarters. It has brought out the good, the bad, and the ugly. In this morning's newspaper I read that eighty one thousand people in Karnataka had suffered from post Covid depression. The main causes are unemployment, fear of contacting the Covid-19 virus, lack of social contact and activity, inability to travel, and be with their loved ones. This brings about worry and anxiety. I realized that the way to beat these evils was to seek joy. To identify and list the things that make me happy. ***Consciously thinking about the things that bring me joy, allows me to notice the positives, amongst the doom and gloom.*** To be grateful for the things I have taken for granted, and appreciate what I have. I spend more time with my wife, which has made me realize the wonderful person, that God had blessed me with, to be my life partner. I read and write more which increases my knowledge and awareness. I eat nutritious home made food, exercise regularly, and follow a regular routine; adding wellness, energy, and freshness to my life. The time available is enjoyably and gainfully spent in learning online the art of speed reading, public speaking, and running a Speakers Forum, on which virtual talks and talent fests are conducted.

My friends tell me that we are losing precious time from our lives in our silver years, and feel frustrated at not being able to travel, and be with their grandchildren. I feel differently. I know that sooner or later the light will surely come. I know my present lifestyle will add several healthy years to my life, and teach me to live and enjoy my life more. I know that finally I will be the winner and overcome the pandemic.

Retirement – Living Beyond the Immediate

*The choice is ours to have the courage
to discover and use our core talent.*

A month before I retired, the farewell invitations started pouring in. It was only then, that the full realization of retiring struck me. I had proudly worn the olive-green uniform at the age of twenty; and since then, for the past four decades, it had become an integral part of my life. It seemed unbelievable that a few days from now, I would be shedding my beloved uniform forever. The cantonment life, the sprawling bungalow with a sentry at the gate, the staff cars, a salute after every hundred yards, the staff in the house, the busy schedules every day, would all be left behind. I would be a retired person with no office, no position, no authority, no powers. I would have all the time in the world, with no dead lines to meet. On the stroke of midnight, on September 30th 2000, I became a retired personnel and a pensioner.

A few days before I was to retire, my personal assistant put up for my signature, the form to be submitted for a retired officers' identity card. In the column 'Color of hair' he had entered 'black and white'! With just one stroke of the pen, he had converted a colorful cavalry officer, to a black and white retired person.

129

On reaching Sena Vihar, Bangalore, my first reminder of being a retired officer was being stopped by a sentry at the Army golf course gate. I was informed, "no entry for retired personnel from this gate" and had to use another gate. After settling down, I was invited by my old friend Maj Gen P R Bose (Retd), for a drink. He asked me in all earnestness whether I would like to take on Vice Presidentship of the 'Sena Vihar Go Getters Club'. On querying what this club was about, he replied with equal earnestness "we are all retired and our wives tell us to go get this and go get that, so we have formed a Go getters Club!"

Shortly thereafter, I was invited to a get together by my retired colleagues to join the retired officer's fraternity. Throughout the evening I was lectured by one colleague after another, that now after working hard for almost four decades, I had earned my right to relax. I should get up late in the morning, play golf for the better part of the day, and in the evening have a drink and gossip. I tried out this relaxation mode for a few months; but deep within, I felt that I was letting my life drift by. I was living by default not by design.

I had always wanted to write and speak on my observations on life and attitudes. I did a course on communication skills and took to public speaking and writing. Since then, I have been happy, busy and gainfully employed. It has also given me the opportunity to travel for delivering talks, see many places, and meet professionals in different walks of life. In my colony I have founded the Speakers Forum. Once a month we have speakers from the colony, speaking on topics of their choice and interest. It affords an opportunity to the residents to spend an enjoyable evening, hearing talks on interesting topics, meeting each other, and socializing over a cup of coffee and snacks.

As I see it, we live our lives in two phases, with the break at the stage of retirement. The first phase of life has to do with ambition, competing, and getting ahead in life. The second phase is more risky because it has to do with living beyond the immediate. If we do not take responsibility for going into the second phase, and organizing our lives so that it is better than the first, we will join the ranks of those who are drifting their way through retirement, which leads to unhappiness. The key to making our retirement happy is to make the shift to doing something significant, something fulfilling. God has given each one of us a core talent, a talent with which we can give back something to this world, however miniscule. We must have the courage to find that talent and live it, so that the world can benefit in some way. It can be making YouTube videos of battles fought, teaching the needy, writing and giving talks, learning yoga, and imparting lessons or anything of our interest. We do not have to be a Mahatma Gandhi, Thomas Edison or Mother Teressa. Just a normal human being, using a core talent, and living life gainfully.

The small acts by the use of our core talent add up to a great life, a successful life, a happy life, a contended life. It fulfils the purpose for which God has blessed us with life. We should live by choice, not by chance. *The choice is ours to have the courage to discover and use our core talent.* To give to ourselves and to the world in retirement something which makes our lives significant, so that we live, not merely exist; so that we strive, thrive and continue to enjoy the best of life; a gift beyond measure, given to us by God.

Zero or Hero

*Life has taught me that it is never too
late for anyone to be a hero.*

He looked like a vagabond, unkept and untidy and every
morning during my walk, I found him cleaning cars. I
noticed he took a lot of care over each car, scrubbing, and
polishing. So, one morning I stopped by to have a chat with
him. His name was Ramesh, he was twenty years old, had
dropped out from school after class eight, since his parents
did not have the money for further schooling. A year later, I
saw Ramesh delivering newspapers to the flats in the
colony, very early in the morning. After distributing the
newspapers, he got down to car washing. After another
year or two, Ramesh had taken another distribution, and
delivered milk. Ramesh was now busy from 5 AM to 11
AM distributing newspapers, cleaning cars and thereafter
distributing milk. He owned an old scooter, which he used
to save time. Next Ramesh took to using his afternoons and
evenings to distribute bottled water.

His appearance was now neat and tidy, his clothes fitted
well, and were clean and pressed. Ramesh got married to an
educated graduate girl of his choice, who was intelligent
and industrious. Our colony has a small shopping arcade,
when a shop fell vacant, Ramesh hired it and set up a
grocery store, after taking a bank loan. His shop was next

to the only other grocery shop in the complex. By his well thought out inventory, courteous behavior, and prompt home deliveries, he won over the complete clientele from the adjoining grocery shop. During the Covid-19 lockdowns in 2020 and 2021, Ramesh went out of his way to help the many elderly people staying in the colony, by attending to their needs and requirements, and endeared himself to all of us. Both he and his wife ran the shop, and Ramesh was now making a good income. From a vagabond, he had transformed his life to a respected and valued young man. Ramesh had gone from zero to being a real-life hero!

A four year old girl was brought from a charity home to my parents' house, saying that she was a destitute, and requesting she be given shelter. She was taken in, and from that day it became her home. My mother named her Mridula, but called her Bapi, and it remained Mridula's pet name. She grew up over the years to be an obedient, disciplined, and dignified girl,studying conscientiously, and even completing her post graduation. Bapi's marriage was arranged with Indresh Verma who was employed with LIC, in the higher pay bracket. Today Bapi and Indresh have their own house, car, a son and daughter who are teenagers and excelling in their studies.

Bapi had come as a destitute girl, and at a young age had the opportunity of living with a good family. My mother was a kind woman who believed in values, principles, discipline, and hard work. Bapi imbibed the same values which changed her from zero to being a heroine in the true sense of the word.

Mumbai is the financial capital of the country. It has the super rich and the poorest of the poor. Ati was born in a super rich family with the proverbial golden spoon in his mouth. He went to a renowned and expensive school, and mingled with the children of the rich and famous. A chauffeur driven Mercedes car dropped and brought him back from school. He had never been in a bus or local train. After finishing school, he was sent to USA for under graduation and post graduation studies. Ten years have gone by since post graduation, but Ati has never worked and earned money. Ati is happy going around the world and living a play boy's life, all on his father's money. His philosophy is that I have everything so why work? Ati was born a hero but became a zero.

Life does not start us off on a level playing field. But life gives us opportunities which if taken at the opportune moment leads to success and fortune. Life does give a choice to each one of us, to shape our own lives by imbibing the right values, principles, and working hard. In my silver years I have realized that in the course of life opportunities will be missed, and mistakes will be made. The years have taught me that it is never too late to make course corrections. It is never too late, and live by the words of Rudyard Kipling's poem:

"If you can keep your head when all about you

Are losing theirs and blaming it on you;"

Life has taught me that it is never too late for anyone to be a hero.

Politics and the Army Man

*We must remember that a nation gets
what it deserves.*

On joining the army, like the Hippocratic oath that physicians take, the army man pledges not to think, speak or hear anything about religion and politics. For the better part of my life, for forty long years, religion and politics were blank pages in my mind. All for a very good reason, because the men we command are drawn from all religions. The places of worship at the units are for all religions, which officers visit and pay homage. For the army man his senior's orders cannot be questioned. The President is the supreme commander and the government of the day lays down the policies and orders. It is for the soldier not to question why but to do or die. So obviously politics is taboo. It is essential to have this bent of mind to enable soldiers to lay down their lives. The army man lives in small cantonments, protected from the turmoil going on in the world beyond his cantonment. In 1975 when emergency was declared in the country, the army man was impervious to the happenings. To him life continued in the same way.

On retirement, I decided to settle down in an army colony to spend my silver years. It was therefore at the age of fifty-six, that I had my first exposure to how my country was governed. Questions came to my mind as to which party would be better suited to govern the State, and which at the Centre. It now became important to have a closer look at the politicians, and the role politics played. In a similar manner, the meaning and practice of secularism in letter and spirit; the use of majority and minorities in politics and consequently, the major role of religion in our lives were unexplored facets. The understanding of different religions, the right and wrong perceptions of one religion by the other, how religious beliefs affected the common man, the role of minorities in our country, and how one community viewed the other had to be learnt afresh.

In retired life I found ample time to indulge in reading and applying myself to questions I did not know enough about. We pride ourselves in being one of the biggest democracies of the world. How many of us have read the Constitution of India, on adopting which, Independent India became a Republic? What exactly, did a democracy mean? There are several definitions of democracy; the often repeated phrase, "government of the people, by the people, for the people" is from Abraham Lincoln's 1963 Gettysburg Address. In effect, we recognize the principle of one man, one vote. But is political democracy enough? We must make our political democracy into a social democracy. What does social democracy mean? Dr Bhimrao Ramji Ambedkar, the man who was the principal architect of India's constitution, emphasized that social democracy is the way of life which recognizes liberty, equality and fraternity. Unfortunately, around me I do not find economic equality, or social equality. There are the extremely wealthy and those who live in abject poverty. To achieve fraternity in a country with several religions and dozens, indeed hundreds of castes and creeds seems like an unlikely proposition. Politics, in reality, is the monopoly of a few, although in theory, it is open to all. To have a vibrant democracy we must have principled leaders and most important of all, knowledgeable and discerning voters.

India is a great country, and to keep it thus, it is the responsibility of us citizens, each one of us, to ensure that we are governed by our best. That can only be achieved if each voter, in whichever walk of life, understands his country, the inherent problems, the weaknesses, and the strengths. Equally important, each individual must understand, and demand his rights. For this, we must have a good government. A good government is formed with good leaders and we are individually responsible to vote into power good leaders. We will be letting down our great country if we even in retirement say with bravado "Oh, I don't get involved in politics and governments." *We must remember that a nation gets what it deserves.*

Will Golf Give Me a Mulligan?

I have learnt that any situation can be overcome with grit, determination, and the will to be cheerful and happy.

For over twenty-five years I have taken innumerable Mulligans on my first tee off. Most were for the better some not. Golf had become an integral part of my life. The earmarked, bi-weekly days for golf were sacrosanct, and all other activities were put on pause. On every occasion, I left with my golf cap jauntily perched on my head, a broad smile on my face, and my wife cheerfully seeing me off and saying in Bengali, enjoy the game come back safe. On every occasion she received me back with a glass of water in her hand, and a smile on her face. The evening prize giving parties were memorable with drinking, back slapping, golfers recollecting the good shots, with joy writ large all over their faces. Two categories of people were automatically qualified as my friends; an ex-National Defense Academy officer and a golfer. The latter were a breed apart, a brotherhood marked by their hugging and swearing. That is why, I had formed and named the golfers club of my colony as "Golfers Breed."

On that day, 12th November, 2018 my wife as usual saw me off with a smile, and said that she had planned a special lunch with me. My first tee off was better than normal and I sailed along merrily chatting and joking with my 4 ball (on that day 3 ball). On the 11th green while coming down a wet, muddy slope I suddenly felt myself being tossed off my feet. The next few hours were spent in a haze of excruciating pain. My wife standing next to the stretcher, before I was wheeled into the operation theatre. I trying to camouflage my pain with a weak smile; but the sad and sorrowful look on her face clearly showed that her agony was many times more than mine.

Seven weeks passed and during that period I realized that time can be used profitably by reading, writing, music. I have realized that those who we treat as our staff are more worthy, than many of those whom we profess to be our friends from our strata of society. I have learnt there are fakes and there are people who stand beside you like a rock in adversity. *I have learnt that any situation can be overcome with grit, determination, and the will to be cheerful and happy.* I have realized that the final say will be that of God. My recovery was slow but well spent. In due course of time, Golf certainly did give me a Mulligan!

The Incredible Mr. Sony

*Money could not bring the happiness,
which relationships could*

I met Sony by mere coincidence. Some meetings in life are predestined. With my penchant of writing, I sit for long hours typing on my laptop. At times my laptop misbehaves, and I am at a loss to put it right. During one such incident, my PA suggested contacting Sony. On the other end of the phone, I heard a warm cheerful voice, and a meeting was arranged for the next day. At the appointed time Sony arrived, a back pack slung around his shoulder and a huge grin on his face. His very presence brightened me up! He worked on my laptop for two hours and during that time, my PA and I had a lively, jovial chat with him. Once the laptop was repaired, Sony got up to leave. When I asked him how much I owed him for his services, he waived me aside and said, "nothing". I was surprised and when I insisted once again, I was amazed by his answer. He said, he had spent a delightful and happy morning chatting with me, and that was more than any payment. Sony left with his happy gait, back pack slung on his shoulders, and a grin on his face.

As time passed Sony and I met and spoke to each other regularly. Sony was a professional computer engineer who had worked in Dubai for several years, and returned to

India, when his mother fell ill. He took a part time job of four hours a day, and in the time available to him thereafter, he spent attending to his ill mother, and sharing quality time with his wife and two children. He also attended two or three clients in a day for computer repairs. Sony gave up a lucrative job because he realized that money was necessary, but relationships were more important. ***Money could not bring the happiness, which relationships could.*** Sony had taken a choice to be happy, make others happy, and was determined to succeed in his chosen path of life.

In the materialistic world of today, position in society is endorsed by power, status, and by money power. Values based on character, integrity, and loyalty are relegated to non-essentials. In Sony, I had met a man who had chosen to keep money in its own place, and spread joy and happiness around him, by nurturing good relationships. A man, who would have a deep impact on the people he met, and spread happiness where ever he went. Undoubtedly the type of people we needed in the world today! I had indeed been very fortunate! I had met the incredible Mr. Sony.

Fifty - Five Years Ago

*Course mates are true friends and
forever willing to help at all costs.*

"Should auld acquaintance be forgot,
    And never brought to mind?
    Should auld acquaintance be forgot,
    And days of auld lang syne?"

To this immortal tune, the Gentlemen Cadets of 36 Indian Military Academy Course are doing a flawless slow march under the flag mast, into the portals of Chetwode Hall. On the wall is engraved the famous words of Field Marshal Philip Chetwode,

"The safety, honor and welfare of your country come first, always and every time.

The honor, welfare and comfort of the men you command come next.

Your own ease, comfort and safety, come last, always and every time."

These words have become immortalized and are the abiding touch stone for all those who have taken the "final step "and believe in the ethos of leadership and soldiering in its purest form." The Indian Military Academy is one of the foremost academies of the world. All those who are blessed to pass out of this institution have the Chetwode Motto etched firmly in their hearts.

On 25th December 1965, fifty five years ago my course mates and I became Officers and Gentlemen. We were young men twenty or twenty one years old, all in the prime of our physical and mental state. All motivated, rearing to go, to win laurels in the noble profession of safe guarding the honor and security of our country. We were ambitious to reach the highest pinnacles of leadership. As Napoleon had said, "every soldier carries a marshal's baton in his knapsack". We had our whole life to look forward to. As dashing 2nd Lieutenants we did not know what the future held and we did not care. All we knew was it is not ours to reason why it is but to do and die, to paraphrase a line from Tennyson in Charge of the Light Brigade. For the past four years we had been together. In January 1962, as sixteen and seventeen year olds, we joined 27 Course at the National Defence Academy and from then onwards we were tied together till death do us part, with that wonderful word "Course mate". Villash Gokhale and Arun Pandit looked at each other in the corridor of the military special train coming from New Delhi to Kirkee. They were both bound for Kirkee going to join the 27th Course at the National Defence Academy (NDA). At the Kirkee station they were told in a firm voice by the Ustad (instructor) to lift the steel trunks and holdalls on their head and proceed to the Shaktiman three ton vehicle. After forty five minutes of being tossed around in the three ton, on reaching NDA they were ordered to go "on the double" to the barber shop immediately and return after looking like a cadet. En route they were stopped by second termer Duke who asked them to give his full name or to keep front rolling till they could answer. They had met Duke for the first time in their life.

That was the mildest form of ragging. From that day on they were transformed from two strangers to course mates for life with loyalty towards each other till the end. Course mate is that magic word which casts a spell where ever you are, in whatever situation you are. A course mate will always help, each and every time.

Now, after passing out from the IMA we would be parting ways. We would be joining our units in different parts of the country. The journey of life had started, and brought to mind Omar Khayyam's lines,

"The Moving Finger writes; and, having writ,

Moves on: nor all thy piety nor wit

Shall lure it back to cancel half a Line,

Nor all thy tears wash out a word of it."

Years went by, we moved on. The 1971 Indo Pak war came and we lost some of our best and some were decorated. The moving finger kept writing. Most of us got married between 1971 to 1973. From daring, fearless bachelors we became mature, responsible, conscientious, husbands. Career took a higher priority and courses were taken seriously. Staff college became a do or die. For the first time there was competition and the concept of first amongst equals emerged. After I returned from senior command course, a friend's wife asked my wife Narayani what grading I had got? Narayani answered in an indignant tone "our husbands are officers they do not get gradings"! Little did she know that we are graded throughout our career. I had married a refreshingly independent and frank girl who never got awed or impressed by gradings, positions or rank. Lucky me! On our name board is written "Chaks & Nanu ". No rank, no decorations. Years went by, some of the very deserving got left behind. Some rose high and a few to the zenith. Some lost their spouse and faced the adversity bravely and squarely. Many succumbed to illness. Course mates kept diminishing with every year. But the spirit remained alive. Whenever we hear of a course mate our eyes light up. ***Course mates are true friends and forever willing to help at all costs.***

On 25th December 2020, fifty five years later, we course mates are seventy five or seventy six years old. We are grandparents and some will be great grandparents in a few years. Life has taught us many lessons. We have learnt that life is not what we have gained or how high we have gone, not about being better than the man next to you; but about relationships built, friendships sealed, kindness and empathy shown towards others. Course mates face the joys and sorrows of life together. They are our true buddies. We are six course mates, Chana, Shimi, Nath, Nagi, Chandran and myself in Sena Vihar, Bangalore. Franklin is across the road in Jal Vayu Vihar. On 25th December we celebrated the remembrance of "Passing Out" together. On that day where ever we are let us all say *Cheers!* to being course mates.

Letter to a Sibling

*Blessed are those families who do not
vie for the gold medal in the races of
life.*

On 13th September 2021, our youngest sibling turned seventy-three. Four of us siblings are blessed to have spent seventy-three long years together without losing any one of us. We spent our childhood years together in the place we treasured the most, our home with our parents. Those were years of fun and frolic in Jabalpur, Pune, Jalandhar, and Delhi. Father being in a transferable service, meant we moved to different boarding schools and met for short periods only once or twice a year. From childhood, to teenage, from school to college, to university, to working lives; we saw more and more of the top, developed our own traits, our own values, and our own characters. Each one of us, set their individual goals and priorities.

When we are young, our family is our parents' family and our relationships are centered on our parents and siblings. Then marriage comes along and we leave our parental home, have our own family, our spouse and our children. Our main relationship shifts from our parents and siblings to our spouse and children. Our siblings similarly move into different homes and relationships. The complexities and races of life begin, by comparing careers and jobs, wealth, performance of children, status, family property, the list is endless. Arrogance, ego, pride, and self-righteousness, find their insidious way in. Relationships are forgotten, selfishness takes over. Families move apart and siblings disown each other. Unless the game is played well by one and all, the results can be disastrous. Blessed are those who can survive the vagaries of life. Blessed are those families who stand together in joy and sorrow. ***Blessed are those families who do not vie for the gold medal in the races of life.***

Now in my silver years, when we have run our races, lived our lives and are in our grace years, I sit back and reflect on the futility of wealth, greed, status, ego, arrogance, jealousy, and self-righteousness. I look back on duties done, and on duties failed. On the importance of relationships; good relationships bind us together and bad relationships shatter us. I reflect on the purpose of life, and on what will remain once we are no more; perhaps, only the love we leave behind. I look at the warmth and love in my wife's eyes when she often speaks of her maternal grandfather (Dadu). I realize the joy and happiness he must have brought to this young girl in her growing years. By bringing such happiness to even one person he would have served his purpose of life in this world. He would have won all the gold medals. I reflect on the happiness brought by forgetting ills of the past, the ability to forget, the strength needed to ask for forgiveness. To forget offences given and taken. Not to leave behind broken relationships, even when grave injustice has been done.

We four siblings are fortunate to be together today, all in our seventies and eighties. We do not know what the morrow brings. Happy birthday my dear sister, may you have many more birthdays, with good health and cheer. God Bless you. Affectionately, Chorda (younger brother).

Bonding Down Memory Lane

We alighted from the bus to the cheers and hugs of our friends! A feeling of elation experienced only very rarely in a lifetime.

For a sixteen year old boy, it is just not difficult, but very nearly impossible, to visualize the next fifty years ahead. Fifty years do seem a very long time, almost a lifetime, when one is young. The announcement of our National Defense Academy (NDA) course Golden Jubilee Reunion on the course social media group, sent me into a state of euphoria, a state of intense excitement and happiness! I immediately made a chart for DLFGJ (days left for Golden Jubilee), much in the same way as we did in our cadet days, when we made charts of DLTGH (days left to go home), before the term holidays. Every day I would strike off one day and feel a growing sense of happiness. My wife sensed my happiness in revisiting the many memories at NDA, and shared my eager anticipation. Staying in the cabins where I had spent three years of my joyful youth. Stepping on to the drill square where as a first termer, I gave my drill test to earn my lanyard. The excitement and happiness at having cleared the drill test in the first attempt. The audience in splits of laughter when I spoke in the auditorium on "Co-education at the NDA", I had no way of knowing it would become a reality fifty eight years on! It was my first attempt at public speaking, and I had no idea that life would come a full circle after retirement, when on the same platform I would address the NDA on 'Attitude', by invitation of the Commandant.

. After a long wait the 14th of December finally arrived. We took the early morning flight, to be able to spend the better part of the day at NDA. On alighting at Pune airport, I was delighted to meet Dilip Roy Chaudhury, Baldev Bhatia, and their better halves. The Non-Commissioned Officer (NCO) at the airport took charge of our luggage and stacked it in the 3-ton vehicle. Memories came flooding back of the time when the NDA special train chugged into the railway station, bringing us first termers to Kirkee station. We had to lift our steel trunks on our heads, pile them into a 3 ton vehicle, and then, jump in! Now, the NCO loaded our luggage, and we climbed into the bus, singing Col Bogey's song, all along the way to NDA.

As we crossed each land mark, we became more and more nostalgic. The riding school reminded us of the jumps in the death lane riding bare back, the inevitable falls, but always reclaiming our mount, encouraged by the Ustads (instructors). Memories of our Air Force friends and their incessant fascination with the gliders; and the Gole market that we made a bee line for on Sundays. As the bus swung into the cadet's mess on the lawns outside, we saw our course mates making merry with beer glasses in their hand. *We alighted from the bus to the cheers and hugs of our friends! A feeling of elation experienced only very rarely in a lifetime.* The next two days were full of merriment and laughter. Recollecting the pranks we had played, and the punishments we had volunteered to share, with a smile! All packed into two unforgettable days!

I have often sat back and reflected on those two eventful and historic days, when we course mates met and spent time together after having joined the NDA fifty years ago. We were then young lads stepping into a career with many plans and aspirations. We wanted to excel, we wanted to compete, and the NDA imbibed in us the healthy way of going about it. On completing our training at the NDA for three years, each of us went our own way. Thereafter some met frequently, some met occasionally, some after long periods, and some only now after a gap of 50 years. After leaving NDA, as the years turned into decades, life's fortune wheel kept moving. Marriage, children, children's marriages and grandchildren. Jet black hair turned silver grey, or to no hair at all! Six pack stomachs transformed to robust beer paunches. Health and bereavement took a toll on some of us. "The Moving Finger writes and having writ, moves on", destiny had played its role. Some attained fame and glory and some fell by the way. Yet, when course mates met, the flame of course spirit was rekindled. In retirement, some had moved ahead into second careers with new jobs. Some had made a name in making YouTube productions, others in writing and publishing. Many had taken to travelling extensively and seeing the world. Some excelled in playing golf, designing golf courses and had become certified golf coaches. Then there were those who had become yoga gurus. A few basked in the glory and fame of their service days. Now fifty years later the course mates were meeting again in the same environment of our training days. We stayed in our cabins, shared wash rooms, ate in the same dining hall. Our wives who stayed with us, were meeting the buddies of their loved ones, with whom they had grown up and become men. The same NDA, the same atmosphere, the same bonhomie, and the joy of reuniting, of being together! The happiness I experienced on meeting my friends Rajvir Yadav, MS Sekhon, Bhat, Pandit, Arun Mishra, Sarge, Mohit Malik, and Kewal Ramani, to mention just a few, cannot be explained in words. The list can go on, and how can I forget my E squadron friend the outspoken, Suresh Datt? But there was a difference, no aspirations, no more the spirit to excel. Life had taught us the meaning of the evergreen song "Que sera sera, whatever will be will be, the future is not ours to see, Que sera sera". The magic mirror where we see ourselves many times a day, day after day, year after year, reflected a mirage, that hid the toll which the years had taken. On coming face to face with so many course mates fractured the mirage. The realization dawned on us that we too had been transformed like our friends, from handsome young men to weather beaten vintage veterans. At seventy, the road ahead could lead to eighty or even longer. Yet, the nostalgia filled days of the Golden Jubilee Reunion has given us something to cherish; indelible memories which we will treasure for the rest of our lives.

Positivity Vaccine

Beyond every dark tunnel there is bright sunshine.

Senior army officers posted to New Delhi, stayed at Sangli Hostel before they moved to authorized accommodation. We were a bunch of eight children all about ten years old. At 5PM every evening we gathered at the park within the hostel to play. Uncle Bardhan also came to the park at about the same time to do his exercises. He was a good natured and jovial person, fond of children. We would often gather around him, to hear him tell us stories. Each story conveyed a lesson for us young children. After all these years a story he told us is still vivid in my mind.

There was a very young officer, a young captain who used visit the physiotherapy department every morning. While his battalion was operating in Mizoram his platoon had been ambushed. Under his leadership they fought bravely and broke the ambush. Unfortunately, a bullet hit him in the spine which left him paralyzed below the waist. He was to be boarded out of the army, and a career he loved brought to a halt. At that time, the young Captain was being treated and rehabilitated. What was amazing about this young man was his high spirits. Nothing could get him down. He had trained his mind to be positive. It was as if he had been vaccinated for positivity. His whole life was ahead and he was determined to make a success of it, to be happy and content. He would never, ever, blame his destiny and fate. He would never let the paralysis in his legs come to his head. Uncle Bardhan brought home to us the tremendous power of positivity. A power, which would stand us in good stead, throughout our lives.

The military hospital next to my house was full beyond capacity, with our soldiers wounded in the action. I visited the hospital frequently and spoke to the men. Some of those critically wounded would say, " saab, mujhe jaldi paltan wapas jana hai, mein bilkul fit huan" (Sir,I want to return quickly to the regiment, I am completely fit). They were the ones who recovered fast. The power of positivity did wonders and the doctors were also amazed.

In 1992 I was commanding a brigade. For Deepa Malik it was her first station after marriage. She was just about twenty years of age, refreshingly young and with a zest for life. A few years later I learnt that Deepa had been afflicted by a disease of the spine which confined her to a wheel chair for life. It was a terrible blow but Deepa refused to accept **defeat. She is the first Indian woman to win a medal in Paralympic Games**. She won a silver medal at the 2016 Summer Paralympics in shot put. She went on to win a gold in F-53/54 Javelin event, at the para athletic Grand Prix held in Dubai in 2018. Deepa was ingrained with positivity. It was as if she had been vaccinated with positivity at birth.

In January 2020, the rumblings of Covid-19 started and were initially not taken seriously. Trump's visit took place and thousands lined the roads. Flights from other countries continued as usual. We took little heed of it and life was more or less normal. By the middle of March 2020, Covid-19 had well and truly taken root in India. On the 24th of March 2020, the Prime Minister of India announced the lockdown. Life came to a standstill and fear crept into our lives, newspapers were full of nothing but frightening news about Covid-19. Negativity was spreading fast and thick, one could not open a TV channel not blaring details on Covid-19. WhatsApp groups were flooded with posts on Covid-19, poisoning our minds with negativity and rumors. Number of cases surged ahead, followed by the terrifying shortage of hospital beds, non-availability of oxygen cylinders, medicines and the ever present spectre of dead bodies lining up for cremation. Our lives centered around Covid-19, Covid-19, and only Covid-19 became the topic of conversation. Over the months fear slowly spread its tentacles deep; depression had set in as we could not travel to foreign countries, to see our children and grandchildren, our most precious ones. Being confined to our homes and not having domestic help brought about weariness and frustration. As more and more time went by, we had to guard against the deadly cocktail of fear psychosis, depression and frustration.

At times like this positivity must be brought to the forefront. My mind goes back to what I have read about the notorious German concentration camps. The few who survived and came back, brought home the point, how their minds helped them to survive those terrible, frightful years. I think about the stories Bardhan uncle told us about positivity, about the paralyzed young captain in the wheel chair, about Deepa Malik's grit and determination. At times like these, when the pandemic played havoc with our minds, we must use all our positivity and strength of mind to fight back. ***Beyond every dark tunnel there is bright sunshine.*** We will definitely defeat Covid-19. Let us fight back with all our strength and positivity of mind. Let us occupy our minds with creativity, by writing, reading, hearing music, learning a new language online, improving our computer skill sets. Let us take the vaccine for positivity!

On Other Side of the Hill

Aging is not decay it is growth.

A few months ago, while driving down Mahatma Gandhi Road, the hub of Bangalore's shopping area, I noticed the many hoardings featuring young and beautiful people. There was a handsome young man featuring a shirt, two beautiful young women smiling over a perfume bottle, a sultry teenager featuring low slung jeans. Not once did I see a hoarding with an aging person. I got a sinking feeling that life only belonged to the young and beautiful. Was I on the other side of the hill?

Over the next few months, I pondered over aging. Slowly another perspective formed in my mind. When we are young we are completely wrapped up with egoistical things like career making, fame, and fortune. We get involved in hundreds of meaningless acts just to get the approval and praise of others. We live by the social mirror of the existing culture, society and the ensuing expectations. When we get older, we look back at our life and say, is this what I really want? Is something missing? As we grow older, we pause, and take time to learn more. If we stayed at thirty, we would always be as ignorant about life as we were at thirty. ***Aging is not decay; it is growth.***

The purpose of life is to accept the realities, make the best of them, and most important, have fun in doing so. Certainly, we cannot ignore the fact of growing old. But attitudes are more important than facts. The attitude with which we approach a fact is all important. The secret of living life is not what happens to us, but what we do with what happens to us.

Our silver years can become a very significant and interesting time in our lives, with the right attitude. What one worries about is not the result of old age; it is brought about by the state of one's mind and one's attitude. One is as old as he thinks he is. Some reach old age at sixty some are living and thriving at eighty.

Our sunset years are not pressed with other engagements. This is the time to do things we have always wanted to do. Read, travel, and write about life. The key is to keep our mind occupied. This can be achieved by continually growing. Learning is a continuous and open ended process. In old age we have to learn to live in changed circumstances. We have to continue to maintain a positive attitude towards life. The right attitude can make life on the other side of the hill, a pleasant affair, until the sun sets on our life forever.

Regimental Life

Regimental life forms an inseparable part of our lives. Friendships are made for a life time.

A comfortable drawing room, a glass of scotch whisky in hand, in the company of regimental officers, and memories of regimental life come flooding back. This is exactly what happened a few years ago at Bangalore when three regimental officers met for a reunion.

In 1966 we were stationed at Sangrur. The Division cross country championship was to be held and all units were required to field teams including one officer. Our Commandant herded all youngsters together, and asked who would volunteer. Paddy, who had never run cross country before, immediately stood up and volunteered. Col Harbans who had taken over the Regiment after a long stint outside was impressed with Paddy's height, and complimented him for volunteering. Kumeresan (Kumi) a cross country blue from the National Defense Academy and the Indian Military Academy, was goaded by us to put his hand up. Seeing Kumi's short height and slight build Col Harbans gave Kumi a severe dressing down for trying to be funny and dismissed the matter. It took a lot of convincing by our Second-in-Command to get the Commanding

Officer (CO) to allow Kumi to run. Needless to say, Kumi came first by a long, long, margin.

Three years later in 1969 we were in Patiala. A young officer was leading the regimental column during an exercise. The radio set 19 crackled with a message that his tank had overrun two buffaloes. A short while later our second in command came on the air to say that he had seen only one buffalo. Where was the second one? Promptly came the reply "Sir, the buffalo is pregnant".

We had all assembled at the Officers' Mess for Sunday beer and lunch. A sing song session followed and Vijay Krishnan was sent in his white herald to fetch Mrs Krishnamurthi (our Commanding Officer) wife's song book from the Commanding Officer's house. After an hour lapsed, Chaks was sent to find out what had kept Vijay so long. Chaks came back with the report that Vijay was found fast asleep in his car with the car resting on one side and the wheels in the air!

Holi was being celebrated at Amritsar in 1984. Adil, Sumer, Anand, Deepak and Soumitra were the younger lot. These youngsters and the ladies were all having a gala time going from unit to unit in a 3 ton. Suddenly there was consternation amongst the youngsters when they found Deepak, fast asleep with his head resting comfortably on the shoulder of the Commanding Officer's wife, after having had one too many beers. Nanu, my wife was sitting quite undeterred, and may even have been contemplating singing him a lullaby!!

Regimental life forms an inseparable part of our lives. Friendships are made for a life time. As life goes on, we lose track of each other and yearn to hear about our friends.

On Turning Seventy Five

...... physical vision would deteriorate
but the added years to our lives clears
our inner vision.

A few days before turning seventy-five in 2019, I received a sum of money sent by the Army Officers Benevolent Fund to my bank. This is a grant given to all officers on completing seventy-five years of age. Amongst some retired officers this is known as the funeral grant. The beginning of the "Sky Gets Dark Slowly", quoted from the title of the book by Zhou Daxin. I take this grant as an incentive to turn eighty when pension goes up by twenty percent. Some take it as a start of having gone to the other side of the hill. For me it is the beginning of the climb to the top of the hill from where the top is visible. The aim being 100 not out.

Well before my birthday my wife and my daughter, my only child, asked me what I wanted as a birthday present. My only wish was that we all be together on that special day. My wife started the birthday celebrations a week before the special day. Seven days of meals I liked. A present for me on all the seven days. My wife and I flew from Bangalore to Hong Kong where my daughter and her family lives and arrived, a day before my birthday. I woke up on 13 September, my birthday, to a bright sunny day with the thought that my remaining life would be as bright and sunny. I had wanted a simple family celebration. Every moment of the day was spent with love and affection showered upon me.

A simple, touching cake cutting ceremony with my eight-year-old grandson taking the lead role. Followed by exchange of gifts. My wife surprised us all with a most imaginative, touching gift, made with a lot of effort - a collage of photos taken through my seventy - five years. The evening was spent taking us through memory lane. My family especially my wife, made me feel the most loved man on, earth. Followed by a sumptuous dinner which we all enjoyed prepared by our Pilipino maid, a par excellent cook. The birthday celebrations continued for the next four days at a luxury hotel at Phuket planned meticulously by my son in law. A memorable landmark birthday full of joy laughter and lovingness. A birthday which confirmed my belief that in the end of our life success is determined not by position, status, money, power but it is relationships which determine how successful our life has been.

The Scottish lady doctor at Mission Hospital Jhansi, who had just delivered me, told my mother with a warm smile "you have a bonny son". That bonny son many seasons later, having weathered the seven seas of life, and many storms, and tides high and low, had just celebrated his 75th birthday. Having lived my life by my own choices like we all do, I now had the finishing point in view. When I leave this world there will only remain the footsteps of my deeds, both good and bad. Time and tide wait for no man and cannot be brought back. My life cannot be re written.

Seventy- five puts one in a different category. My club subscription went down to half. On many golf courses I was entitled to tee off from the over seventy-five line. People offer you their seats in buses. In hospitals there is no que for registration. In many countries, flower shows, exhibitions, heritage buildings have no entrance fees. Travel and entertainment have concessions.

It appears that the world recognizes that you have done your bit and have earned the right to be pampered. Till now the younger generation called you uncle. It seems that almost overnight you have earned the title of Dadu. The silver-grey hair gives a distinguished look to your personality and that little paunch is acceptable. Most important your spouse most happily and lovingly accepts you in any shape or size! A visit to the ophthalmologist declared me as requiring cataract operation. My eyes were losing vision. *I remembered that my mother often said physical vision would deteriorate but the added years to our lives clears our inner vision.* The earlier years flash back clearly. Our values, our priorities, mistakes, false ego, taking ourselves too seriously, living in our past glory, ignoring people who cared for you and giving importance to those who merely used you.

In my block on the same floor just one apartment away in flat no 437 lives Alston John Guria Toppo. A long name for a small boy of seven years. Alston and I met when he was only two years of age, five years ago. From the time we met, Alston and I liked each other instinctively. As the years went by, we spent many a time chatting to each other sitting on our building parapet wall. The innocence, goodness, curiosity, happiness, purity of Alston reminded me of my childhood days. I learnt again from him the actual meaning of life. How the rat race of life had pitched me into the need to prove to myself that I was better than the man next to me. I forgot that true nobleness came from improving my own self.

With seventy-five years behind me and having ample time to myself, my inner vision was opening doors which had been shut for long.

I often notice that I walk much slower than I earlier used to. When alighting from an aircraft and walking towards immigration I am left far behind. On the golf course I get tired after playing nine holes. The spirit is willing, but the flesh feels weak. With age will come ailments.

- ❖ Our attitude will determine the quality of our lives for the remaining years, therefore:
- ❖ Do we give up on our failing health physically and mentally or do we find ways and means of keeping active to the extent possible?
- ❖ Do we indulge in self-pity or make the most of life to the very end?
- ❖ Do we live or merely exist?
- ❖ Do we keep our attitude positive?
- ❖ Do we keep taking steps to overcome our dependence?
- ❖ Do we keep enjoying the musical dance of life which is the gift God has given us?

I believe that we live by CHOICE and not by CHANCE. The choice is ours to take.

My Friend, My Colleague Subi

*That again was our Subi, ever warm
and friendly, always helpful and
generous!*

It was cold breezy morning in December 1969, in Patiala. Punjab can be cold, very cold, in winter. Over a hundred officers had assembled outdoors on the banks of a canal to appear for the Part C practical examination. The Centre for 1 Armoured Division was in Patiala, and officers had come from Sangrur, Nabha, Ambala. There were six points where a major at each point was to conduct the tests. We were distributed into six squads, one for each point. A young, slim, smart artillery officer came and sat next to me as we waited for our individual turn. He put out his hand and introduced himself as Capt N Subramanyam, from 1 Field Regiment of 1 Artillery Brigade, Ambala. He had a firm hand shake, a booming voice, and I instinctively liked him. That was the very first time Subi and I met. Without wasting anytime, he came to the point. I saw your black beret and the Directing Staff who is to take our test is also from the Armoured Corps. This is open plains terrain so a number a of questions are likely to be based on armour tactics. Till our turn comes, can you please tell me the finer points of basic troop and squadron level tactics. That is of course, if you do not mind. Subi's turn came after half an hour and before mine. I saw him walking up confidently to the Directing Staff.

At 1.30PM we were in the buses returning to our different Officers Mess. Subi came and sat next to me in the bus, and in the course of the conversation, he mentioned, he had not seen an armoured regiment officers mess. So, I invited him to have lunch with me in my mess, the 16 Light Cavalry Officers' Mess. Before lunch we walked around the oldest and senior most armoured regiment Mess with a silver goblet of chilled beer. I can still see the interested look in Subi's eyes as I showed him the silver cups squashed in Queta earthquake, the framed parade state of the regiment of January 1776, and the array of battle honours won. In the library Subi spent over half an hour reading through the old newspaper cuttings of the army officer and cricketer Surendra Nath, especially the 1959 England Test Match. That was Subi, always interested in what caught his attention. He asked questions, and wanted to know everything. After lunch I dropped him on my scooter and by then we were friends.

In Sep 2000 I retired and came to settle down in Sena Vihar. One afternoon my wife Nanu came to play Mah-jong and I, to revive my hand at bridge, in the Sena Vihar Institute. In those days, we had a lovely Institute. As I walked into the bridge room, I heard an unmistakable and booming voice greeting me, "Chaks from 16 Light Cavalry!" After several decades Subi had recognized me and the warmth in his voice was palpable. *That again was our Subi, ever warm and friendly, always helpful and generous!* This is what had endeared Subi to each and every one of us in Sena Vihar. I sure was happy to have Subi with me in Sena Vihar!

Subi was best known as a bridge player of extreme dedication and skill. Come rain, hail or storm, every afternoon at 2.30 PM Subi was seated at the bridge table. He was very vocal and loud in his criticism, and many a time had his partner cringing from the Bofors gun volley! But he never meant any harm. Being extremely optimistic by nature, Subi always wanted to play every hand, and always bid a minimum small slam!!!

Subi took ill with his kidneys malfunctioning. I was at the Manipal hospital on a routine yearly check-up when I saw Subi in a wheel chair admitted to the hospital. His morale was high, Subi's morale could never be low! Subi returned to Sena Vihar but his health failed fast. Every evening at 5 pm, I met him on the wheel chair outside G block. By then he knew he was going. He could hardly talk, but remained brave till the end.

I lost my slim, smart, warm friend whom I had met when we both had just five years of service. Years will pass, but Subi will live on in our hearts in Sena Vihar. Subi has been a big loss to all of us but most of all to Rama his charming wife. *Adieu my Friend!*

The Wired World

I want to live in a simple world, a slow world, a free world. I want to recover what I have lost.

My neighbour in Bangalore lives in flat no 4 and coincidently my daughter's flat in Hong Kong is also no. 4. The similarities go further, small nuclear families, an only child under ten with the husband and wife in early forties, working in high profile and well paid jobs. Each couple employs an efficient full time live in maid, who looks after the child and housework. Only branded clothes, house full of the most expensive gadgets, most of them hardly used. Child's room overflowing with expensive toys played with just once or twice, and then discarded. Five star holidays to exotic destinations during Easter, Summer and Winter school breaks. String of couriers with food parcels coming on Sundays, which is maid's day off.

My wife and I live a me for you, and you for me life. We spend eight months in our Bangalore flat. The remaining time is spent with my daughter, son in law and grandson in Hong Kong, and in our travels both in India and abroad.

During my working life I was so engrossed in work, that I did not realize that a world existed outside my work place and home. After retirement my friends advised me to accept job offers coming in. My best friend, my confident, clear headed, outspoken spouse, who always only wanted my happiness, said that I should do what I wanted and approval from others should never be sought. Though advise from others should certainly be considered but finally you must always follow your own judgement. So, I decided to be self-employed, doing what I most wanted. Seeing, observing the whole big world around me, and concentrating on human behaviour. No, do not get me wrong it was not to put my nose in other people's affairs. My choice is to be observant, and form my impression of human behaviour. After all, human behaviour shapes the world. Over the years the empires of the Mughals or Romans were shaped and based on the behavioural traits of the rulers. Aurangzeb was a merciless ruler, while, Akbar was a benevolent Emperor. Today Trump and Modi will chalk out the course of their individual nations, parents shape the family, spouses affect each other and peers influence the growing years of children. Our times and environment have a great impact on our behaviour and in turn, impact our lives. As time went by, I found this new found hobby had turned into a full time occupation. It helped me to put my impressions down as articles. The impressions as articles were to be published, delivered as lectures or presented and discussed in seminars and workshops. Slowly I found myself busy writing and speaking more and more on "Attitudes and Life",

Well, well, where did I start from? Yes, of course, my neighbour's flat and my daughter's flat both no 4. Both with striking resemblances. Take a quick look at their work day. Wake up early morning and drink coffee. Get ready, hurried good byes to dear husband, rush out of the door munching a sandwich or a fruit in hand. Child in tow, to be dropped at school, enroute. Spouses return after eight at night, attempting to spend quality time with the little one, who has been fed dinner by the maid. Office moods often spilling over onto the dining table, laptops out after dinner, work till midnight, and finally retire for the day. A picture that may be a little exaggerated, but by and large, true.

The precious twenty four hours of each day, carved up, dissected and reduced to twenty, thirty minutes segments of efficiency. There is always a sense of urgency to make every moment count. It permeates our thoughts, our daily routines, our meals, our vacation time, and our relationships. Urgency even in saving that fraction of a section by murdering a language by using a "ur" or "coz" This ethos of schedule and speed has penetrated even the lives of our youngest children. Parents feel they must identify what their children are most talented in by the time they are five, or six years of age, to make sure they practice the necessary skills to excel in that field. Children are put into as many as four to five activities during any one time to ensure their success in life. Gone are the days when in the early fifties, I used to wander home from school in Poona, through shortcuts, watching squirrels chasing each other, run after colorful butterflies fluttering in the air.

This transition has been brought about by the speed of communication. Advance in technology has led to the internet, social media, in one word, the Wired Grid. Technology, media, internet has increased the speed of communication to unimaginable extents. This in turn has increased productivity at Sputnik speed at the workplace.

More productivity, is more money. Hence the equation, time is money. People will spend less time on leisure activities when their work time becomes more and more profitable. Technology and economic progress have not increased leisure time, but have achieved just the opposite.

A transformation so very vast, that it has altered all that we say, think and do. The world today is more scheduled and less patient, with an inherent frenzied pace of life. On the roads the honking is incessant and in the dentist's clinic a wait for ten minutes causes immense irritation. As I get off the aircraft in Hong Kong, I find people rushing towards the immigration as if every second counts, although the queue actually stretches to just a few travelers. This enormous transformation has happened in my lifetime from the 1950s when I was a young boy till date. Yet it has been so subtle that we are hardly aware of it. Fifty years ago, internet did not exist, and twenty-five years ago, Google did not exist.

Technology has brought with it many advantages that translate into more productivity and consequently more money. We are richer, have more and better cars, gadgets, iPhones, iPads, iPods, microwaves, air conditioners, dish washers, copying machines and a host of other necessities and luxuries. Most importantly, technology enables instant audio-visual connection to our near and dear ones, who may be miles away.

What have we lost? By slow, almost imperceptible degrees our world has been transformed, we have lost time needed for contemplation, and the open spaces in our minds. We have lost the knowledge of who we are, and what is important to us. All this is happening so gradually, and imperceptibly that we have failed to notice its advance. It is as if we have gone blind and deaf, and given our consent without question. Maybe, we are afraid that non acceptance may earn us the tag of not moving with the times, of being stagnant. Has technology put us in an invisible cage? Forwards are the fashionable "in" thing. Not a single original thought. Is our creativity being threatened by the Wired World? *I want to live in a simple world, a slow world, a free world. I want to recover what I have lost.*

When Friends Meet

The war clouds of the 1965 Indo – Pak war had just receded from the Indian horizon. The country was grappling with the after math of war and the reinduction of troops had started. My Regiment, the 16 Light Cavalry the oldest and the best armored regiment which had led the advance of 1 Armoured Division across the Indo – Pak border in the western sector, was now at Gang village in Pakistan waiting to be reindicted to India. On being commissioned on 25th December, 1965 (Christmas Day), I joined the Regiment in early January 1966 in Pakistan. It was then that I first met AKG, Wendy Dewan, JP Singh, and BM Kapur. We all got together in March 2022 at the Wellington Gymkhana Club as part of the Tally Ho group in the salubrious climate of the Nilgiris to celebrate our friendship of over fifty five years. Jessie a much younger breed of spirited regimental officer joined the group of Tally Ho.

In April we crossed the border and went back to India and camped for three weeks at Janglot under a grove of trees. We were waiting for the rolling stock to load the tanks and go to our peace area station Sangrur. There being no officer's mess in Sangrur we settled for two bungalows to be our residential quarters. Rooms were shared, we ate together, went to the tank garages together and had drinks together in the off duty hours. We were young all in our very early twenties. In the prime of life with six pack stomachs, handsome and dashing cavalry officers. We learnt our soldiering together, played games together, partied together and laughed and learnt to live life to the fullest. The seed of our friendship was sown at that time.

The initial years were spent in the regiment and friendship blossomed. Thereafter, we went our own ways on staff postings, instructional courses, and ERE tenures, with stints of regimental tenures in between. Years went by and the moving finger writ and having writ moved on. We attended each others weddings and revived memories. All of us became a happy lot. Children and grand children came along. The years brought success and failure, ups and downs of life, but our friendship never faltered and grew from strength to strength.

Time kept moving and we hung up our spurs and settled in our own nests, as veterans and senior citizens. We spent our time with our children settled in India and abroad, and played with and pampered our grandchildren. Occasionally we remembered our regiment and our friends, and longed for the good old days, especially the Sunday dosa lunches at the officer's mess. It was during one of these moments that the idea of getting together was suggested. There was a spontaneous agreement to the proposal. At that time Chaks and Nanu were spending a holiday at the Wellington Gymkhana Club, their favorite haunt in the Nilgiris to spend some quiet moments together. The two were given the responsibility of organizing the meet. The location selected for the meet was Wellington Gymkhana Club, and the month of Mar 2022 was decided as the best month in the Nilgiris. Chaks swung into action and helped in booking the cottages in the Club. 14th to 18th March was scheduled for the meet. Air tickets were purchased and Tally Ho waited for the moment to arrive.

Everyone reached the Club by lunch time on the 14th. We gathered at the reception where the receptionist Lata efficiently checked us all in. Back slapping and hugs going around. Six packs had vanished, jet black hair to salt and pepper hair or no hair. From the reception we trooped into the Club dining room for a tasty Chinese lunch. After lunch we continued our catching up at the Gazebo sipping hot Nilgiri tea. We spoke of our days in the regiment. The fun we had playing Holi together, and the regimental day celebrations. Stories of our children growing up together, asking about their present where abouts, seeing photographs of our grandchildren. We grieved for regimental officers and men we had lost over the years.

The Tally Ho group was complete.

Wendy and Neelam

Give Wendy a TV sports channel and a sports magazine and he will be happy for the whole day.

JP and Nilam

Have JP around and a party will never be dull with his stock of party jokes.

BM and Gunmala.

BM always full of fun with his puns and leg pulling.

Chaks and Nanu.

Chaks always the 'Chupe rustom'.

Jessie and Kavita

The youngest amongst us. Their ever willing spirit to help and kindness won us over.

Although in a wheelchair Gen AKG's spirit to participate was a source of inspiration to all of us. Madhu Singh (Madie, 4 H), Nilam and JP's sister in law hosted a fabulous lunch in her out of the world house in Coonoor.

Those four days were like a family reunion. Each day's activities was chalked out carefully, the menus meticulously prepared, outings for shopping planned, and time to rest in between as age was catching up. The 15th March lunch was at the 19th. That night a barbecue dinner was organized at the Club. The 16th March had cocktails and lunch at Savoy, and in the evening Gen AKG was hosted to a sit down dinner at the Club. On the 17th of March a cocktail was hosted by AKG bringing a great reunion to a grand close.

On the 18th Mar all twelve of us were in the dining room at 9 AM to have breakfast and say farewell till we met again. Chaks sprang a surprise with a memento presentation ceremony. An informal group photo had been framed overnight and was presented to each one of us as a remembrance of the wonderful four days spent. It was a touching moment. Memories would linger on. God willing the Tally Ho would meet again.

TALLY HO - 14TH TO 18TH MARCH 2022
WELLINGTON